The Boy in the Statue
From Wartime Vienna to Buckingham Palace
by Sir Erich Reich
ISBN: 978-1-9997646-2-3

Published by

i2i Publishing. Manchester
www.i2ipublishing.co.uk

'Kindertransport – The Arrival'
The small boy with the violin is modelled on a picture of Sir Erich as a boy

World Jewish Relief & the
Association of Jewish Refugees
have the utmost pleasure in announcing
that the new commemorative sculpture

'Children of the Kindertransport'

is now standing proudly at the newly named

HOPE SQUARE

Liverpool Street Station, London EC2

Cast in bronze by the renowned Israeli artist,
Frank Meisler, the sculpture will stand as a
symbol of hope for all those who are
subject to persecution and intolerance.

Photograph courtesy
of John Chase
September 2006

WORLD JEWISH RELIEF   AJR

July 2001. My nephew Michael Reich and I at Birkenau concentration camp at the end of our cycle challenge from the Brandenburg Gate to the gates of Auschwitz

I lost both my parents to the Holocaust.

I was just four years old when I arrived in England.

I never saw them again.

This is my story…

8

Chapter One

A story I started to write about a year before this unveiling and has taken a further thirteen years to finish! I began when alone for several hours 35,000 feet above sea level, hurtling towards the land of my ancient ancestors on my way to Israel to visit my Aunt Irene, the last, then ailing, sibling of my mother and her only sister. Having played such an important role in my life, perhaps she, Auntie, acted as the spur. Or maybe the many twists and turns my life has taken from babyhood to the present instilled in me a need to record it.

Or maybe my two youngest sons, Jonathan and Joel, have to bear some responsibility for my decision to write. When they were young and we were on the dreaded school run I would regale them with tales from my past - a sure way of keeping them quiet, or keeping them apart if an argument was brewing. One or the other would pipe up: 'Dad, why didn't you tell us that story before?'

The boys always seemed genuinely intrigued by my stories, even if they had already heard some of them. Having the oldest dad in the class, and a living relic of World War Two, obviously had its compensations. I remember the time Jonathan came home and proudly told me that during their history lesson on life during the Second World War the teacher had suggested they ask their grandparents what it had been like. My son put his hand up and announced, 'I'll ask my dad!'

I never spoke much about my past when my three older children were growing up although I did discover that my eldest son, Allon, at some point in his youth, used to embellish my Israeli military achievements, of which more later.

I was born in central Europe on the 30th April 1935 in the city of Vienna, the capital of a vast sprawling empire filled with a multitude of cultures and languages. A city that was a magnet for immigrants and refugees, many of whom came from the east. Amongst the many Jews fleeing from pogroms and anti-Semitism around 1915/6 to Vienna was my maternal grandfather, Joshua. He was born Schije Dresner but the name was changed to Splitter in 1925. He was born in Podgorze, a Jewish district near Cracow which, in 1941, would become the ghetto. It is the exact location portrayed in Thomas Keneally's novel *Schindler's Ark*, later adapted by Spielberg for his film *Schindler's List*. The book and film refer to a Mrs Dresner hiding under the stairwell.

My parents, brothers and I, at Zbonzyn May 1939

Vienna is a beautiful city renowned for its culture, architecture, galleries and museums, for its artistic and intellectual citizens. But it was also part of an empire full of internal unrest.

There were Jews in Vienna as early as 1194 and the population grew until 1420 when Albert V ordered the annihilation of the city's Jews, a pattern that has been repeated for the Jewish population of many 'civilised' cities throughout the ages. They were allowed back in, albeit with serious restrictions, until the second expulsion in 1669.

From 1736 a small Sephardic community existed in Vienna which led to a much larger influx with Joseph II's Edict of Tolerance in 1782.

The revolution of 1848 resulted in several changes and the easing of conditions. For the first time Jews had unrestricted rights to live and practise their religion in any part of the country. As a result, the Jewish population in Vienna grew rapidly from just over six thousand in 1860 to forty-two thousand by 1870 and by 1923 had expanded to over two hundred thousand, some ten per cent of the city's total population.

The contribution the Jewish population made in the spheres of art, science and finance well into the twentieth century was disproportionate to the number of Jews living in the city. One has only to recall names such as Barany and Loewi who won Nobel prizes for medicine or Freud and Adler in the field of psychology. And Mahler and Schoenberg who continued the musical tradition of Austria. Not to speak of literature with writers like Zweig and Werfel. Unfortunately, this dominance in the scientific and cultural life of Viennese society brought with it ever-increasing anti-Semitism. Whether this was as a result of pure envy or a more complex mixture of other historic factors is hard to fathom.

It was in this city that my parents, of Eastern European background and traditions, made their home.

I have no recollection of my family or of Vienna – my information comes in the main from my eldest brother Jacques who at the time we were forced to leave the city was himself only eleven years old. We lived in Area 2 of the city not far from the Prater Park, at the time a very Jewish quarter, not extremely religious but of a traditional orthodox background.

My maternal grandparents, it seems, were already fairly assimilated and not particularly religious. My grandfather, having opened a small factory for handmade leather shoes, had become reasonably well off. My father, Schapse Reich, on the other hand, was religious to the extent that he even served as a stand-in cantor during the high holidays. I suppose, having come to Vienna much later and from a very observant family, his outlook on life was somewhat different to that of my mother's family.

Jacques frequented the local synagogue with my father but told me he wasn't particularly keen on the Rabbi. My mother, Mina, on the other hand was apparently not averse to shopping in the local chemist on a Saturday.

Schapse was a salesman basically selling on the 'never, never', so he was away from home most of the week, always returning on a Friday for Shabbat. Frequently we had another guest, Auntie. I'm not sure whether she came because at her home there was no Friday night meal or she was there to help her older sister, Mina, my mother, with her three young children. Much later I found out that Auntie would often hold me as a baby to try and calm me down.

The first years, I suspect with the help of my grandfather, we seem to have been relatively comfortable financially, to the point that we even had a nurse to look after the children. Unfortunately, my middle brother Ossie contracted diphtheria at an early age which then spread into osteomyelitis with serious consequences years later.

The older two boys were sent to a marginally religious camp, 'Barak', during the school holidays. We apparently had a family holiday in the spa town of Bad Ischl, although, again, I have no memory of this. Anyway, despite growing anti-Semitic feelings throughout Austria in general and Vienna in particular, my brother Jacques says he did not sense this attitude towards him or our family.

The dramatic change occurred with the Anschluss in 1938 which saw the annexation of Austria into Germany by Hitler in March of that year, thus bringing the country under his control. Anti-Semitism became far more prevalent. Jewish shops were closed, Jewish academics were barred entry to their professions and my brothers had to change schools. I suppose one of the most demeaning laws was forcing Jews to clean roads with brushes. It seems that my father, despite fierce protestations from the family, went to see what was happening. On returning home unharmed he was asked how that was possible. His reply was, "I told them that if they were prepared to clean the streets in Warsaw I would wash the streets of Vienna. Those louts were so surprised they just let me go."

One day in early 1939 the police knocked on our door and handed my father papers expelling him from Austria as he still had a Polish passport. Recently I asked the archives in Vienna whether they still had the papers relating to this deportation of my father. The reply came back that he was in fact expelled not deported, although I am not altogether sure what the difference is. Very few children were included in the deportation — it was mostly adults. My mother did have an Austrian passport and so could have stayed in Vienna with her children, but, I presume not wanting to be apart from us, Schapse revalidated his Polish passport and came back to Vienna to pick up his wife, me and Ossie, and Jacques from Berlin, and then took his family back to Zbaszyn on the Polish side of the border.

I cannot understand how a wonderful city like Vienna could have such a dark, cruel side, with such hatred toward some of its own inhabitants. It's as if none of the many positive elements of Viennese history and society rubbed off on the local population. I don't often go to Vienna but each time I do the city seems to have a hold on me. I don't remember living there or have any personal recollection of what they did to us and Jews like us who never caused them any harm.

Chapter Two

Vienna to Dorking   Aged 4

Across the fields of yesterday
He sometimes comes to me
A little lad just back from play
The lad I used to be.

T.S. Jones

There is a delightful corner in the south of England through which flows, even if at times only as a trickle, the tiny River Mole. Protecting this beautiful, natural environment are the North Downs and the Greensand Hills whose peaks, Box Hill and Leith Hill, dominate the region. They maintain a sleepless watch over those living in their shadows. At the centre of the valley is the small market town of Dorking, of which Sheridan once wrote, 'The nicest place, within a prudent distance of Town [London] in England.'

It was after the Romans built their military road from the coast to London that settlements began to develop at various resting points along its path. One such, later mentioned in the Domesday Book, was the Manor of Dorchinges (Dorking). For a short while Dorking became an important staging post on the Turnpike Road to Brighton. Since then it has remained a quintessentially English town, set in the midst of inspirational countryside, mentioned frequently by literary figures who have either lived in, or passed through, that land.

The 17th century novelist Daniel Defoe, referred to the lovely Dorking Deepedene Gardens, whilst Jane Austen marvelled at the beauty of Box Hill. In *Emma*, she wrote, 'Emma had never been to Box Hill. She wished to see what everybody found so well worthwhile seeing. Seven miles were travelled in expectation of enjoyment and everybody had a burst of admiration on arriving.'

In *Pickwick Papers*, Dickens mentions Dorking as a wonderful place to stop for a decent pub lunch, and Keats, staying at the Burford Lodge Hotel on the slopes of Box Hill, found time to write, 'O, thou woulds't joy live in such a place.'

I, on the other hand, nearly broke all the bones in my body sledding down this famous Box Hill, one beautiful winter's day. Luckily the giant oak that got in my way hit only the side of my sledge, causing me to tumble into a wet, white blanket of snow which didn't quite drown out my friends' peals of laughter as they peered down at me.

In fact, all of my early memories are of living in Dorking. My boyhood games, my quarrels and accidents, my childhood joys. But the memory which dominates them all came in 1946.

While outside and playing alone, as I often did, on the street where I lived, I was absorbed in my favourite game of make-believe with my little wooden scooter. Always ambitious, I had transformed it into a big red double-decker bus and was busily engaged as the bus driver. I don't know if I had any passengers, but I could easily have imagined a crowded coach. Perhaps, even then, I had premonitions of my future life as a travel organiser. I certainly had no premonition of what was about to happen.

17

A young man with a bike in tow walked up to where I was playing and asked me whether I knew where Mr and Mrs Kreibich lived.

'Of course,' I replied.

My name was not Kreibich, but Emilie and Joseph Kreibich were, as far as I was concerned at that time, my parents.

With my foster-parents Emilie & Joseph Kreibich

I took him the few yards to the front door of a building called Burchett House, and showed him the stairs inside. I told him to go up the stairs and knock on the door of the room at the top. I then ran back out to the street and turned my attention back to transporting the masses of Dorking to some exotic, far-off location.

My 'bus' was somewhere between Jack the Blacksmith striking the hour at Abinger Hammer's famous clock and the Gomshall Saw Mill, with my imaginary busload of passengers, when I heard my 'mother' calling me excitedly.

I transformed my bus back into a scooter and hurried over to her. She was standing with the young man who had asked me for directions. Did she pause before breaking the news to me? Did she realise how my whole world was about to change? I don't know. She simply said, 'Erich, this is your brother Jacques. He wants to talk to you.'

I can only imagine I must have been shocked. And confused. Leading to the start of understanding that my 'family' were in fact my foster family, that the Kreibichs were not my 'real' parents and in time that I was Jewish.

So hard even now to comprehend what it must have been like for me as an eleven-year old boy.

I learned that Jacques was my eldest brother, seven years my senior, and that I had another brother, Ossie, who was six years older than me. After that monumental day, I met up with both my brothers several times and I remember Ossie made the journey to visit me in Dorking. Somehow, despite the intervening years of separation, a new bond was created and we became brothers again, even if not as close as those who have lived their whole lives together as one family.

I honestly can't recall whether the question of our parents came up then or at some other time. I couldn't remember them anyway, and Jacques would hardly have wanted to raise such a painful subject. In fact, the whereabouts of our parents remained hidden for many years, and even after the subject was eventually broached it was rarely discussed; each one of us, no doubt, preferring to retain whatever memories we had in the solitude of our own thoughts.

I have always had the view that recalling the past had a far greater effect on my brothers than on me. I had blocked out what went before and for me life began, for all intents and purposes, not in the city of my birth, Vienna, but in Burchett House, Dorking.

I can't remember when or how I arrived at this rather imposing building. I do, however, quite clearly recall sleeping with other children in a dormitory for several months. Eventually all the others seem to have found families to stay with. The Kreibichs found me. The house was big, certainly in my eyes, with several flights of stairs which we would run up and down, play hide and seek on, and sometimes even slide down the banisters. Not only did it have a large front driveway but the back garden was enormous — a children's haven in the summer — a place to play and lose oneself.

I think there were about twelve refugee families living in the house. Each family had a room in which they lived, cooked and slept. There was only one bathroom and toilet on each floor so it is unlikely I had a proper bath more than once a week, if that.

There was a communal kitchen downstairs, used on a first-come, first-served basis by all the refugees. This would have been the kitchen that served the aristocratic family that normally occupied the house. At this time, it was owned by the Duke of Newcastle who had offered Burchett House rent-free as a hostel for refugees.

Not long after my arrival I was sent to primary school and Emilie, my foster mother, would take me even though the school wasn't that far away. Later I used to walk on my own, dilly-dallying the whole way. How I managed to communicate with the English children there, given that I only spoke German to start off with, I will never understand. They must have taken pity on me because apart from the odd fight or so I quickly became part of the gang. The school itself, still there today, was behind the fire station and not far from the shelters which we visited regularly during the war.

Over the years, I learned something of what had happened to us as a family and as a people. Here's what I now know, although to this day I can't remember any of it.

My father, Schapse Reich, was born in the small town of Ulanov, which is now part of the Ukraine. He was the youngest of nine. Recently I found a picture of my paternal grandfather with his six sons. It was difficult to comprehend that those very religious-looking men were indeed my family. My father apparently met my mother in Vienna whilst on his travels through Europe. She, Mina Splitter, the oldest of six, began her life in the very Jewish town of Oswiecim, later to become one of the most notorious names of the Holocaust – Auschwitz. Both were religious, living strictly according to the laws of Moses and the Bible. Although both Polish, they lived in Vienna and had three boys, Jacques, born in 1928, Ossie, born a year later and, finally, me, little Erich, the baby of the family, born in 1935.

By 1938 I was three and by all accounts Vienna was enjoying a warm early spring, one of the most beautiful and romantic periods of the year: the season of hope, renewal, light and freedom; a time to contemplate nature's forthcoming colours, prolonged daylight and an ever-warming sun.

What better moment, then, for Herr Hitler to start his rampage across Europe? One of his first targets was the country of his birth, Austria, and its capital Vienna, annexed to Germany with the Anschluss. That civilised city received him with open arms and glistening eyes. His was a hero's return; the knight in shining armour, come to save the Germanic races from destruction by the Hebraic and gypsy devils. He was about to create a new order. After all, would this not prove a remedy for all their ills, imagined or otherwise?

Siegfried in all his glory arrived to seduce Brunhilde and give birth to a modern super-race. More akin, I suspect, to *The Rape of Lucretia*. Well, he succeeded beyond his wildest dreams, ushering in a new era. Not so much a super-race but an evil one that extended the boundaries of atrocities far beyond those previously known to mankind.

Poland watched quite happily from the side, little appreciating the ultimate consequences. The Third Reich's brand of racial discrimination no doubt appealed to its own historic philosophy and prejudices. In the autumn of 1938, just as the days were shortening, the air turning decidedly colder and the leaves beginning their annual downward spiral, the Polish government, in its infinite wisdom, decreed that all Polish citizens of Jewish origin residing abroad must return and have their passports revalidated or risk losing citizenship. This affected my parents directly as my father was a Polish citizen and living in Vienna.

What a wonderful plan! The Germans naturally accepted the idea whole-heartedly, turning it to their own advantage and self-interest. Within days of the announcement they rounded up over five thousand families, expelling them unceremoniously to the small Polish border town of Zbaszyn, including my father.

How the pendulum of history swings. One minute fleeing, the next being forced back to the same place. At the end of the First World War, with the crumbling of the old Austro-Hungarian Empire, citizens living in any part of that territory under Habsburg rule were allowed free entry into Austria and Germany. Thousands of Jewish families like my own took the opportunity to seek a better life, away from the dreaded pogroms that had been the hallmark of Poland for centuries. Now, just twenty years later, and having settled in their new home, they were being deported back to the country from which they had fled, trying to escape persecution.

An intrinsic part of Jewish history, I suppose. Not much has changed since Moses led the children of Israel on a forty-year desert escapade. We're still wandering around, looking, searching for a safe haven.

The Polish people weren't exactly enamoured of this turn of events. I doubt if they had envisaged the return of those same citizens they were so pleased to be shot of two decades earlier. The result was that thousands of cold, hungry and homeless families, deprived of their belongings, were initially left stranded on the border between Poland and Germany (which, since the Anschluss of course, now included Austria). The Poles wouldn't let them in and the Germans stopped them from returning. One of many trivial border incidents, you could say, except that this one had a sting in its tail.

Not only was it the first of its kind in modern times but, far more interesting, at least historically, was that amongst those shepherded to no man's land was a certain Mr Grynszpan. His seventeen-year-old son was at the time studying in Paris. Grynszpan Jr. was so incensed at the German treatment of his father that he spent the last of his money on a revolver and twenty-five bullets, walked to the German consulate and asked to speak to an official about his German residency. He was shown in to see a young diplomat called Ernst vom Rath, pulled out his gun and shot Rath five times in the stomach. Rath died two days later.

In Germany, all hell broke loose. It was the perfect opportunity; the Nazis went on an unprecedented rampage, now known as the infamous *Kristallnacht*. Nothing was sacred. It was a free for all, allowing the Aryan master race to show its true colours by defacing and destroying anything remotely Jewish. A night never to be forgotten, and one that left an indelible mark on all those who suffered the terrible consequences.

Meanwhile, for my family and others on the border in Zbaszyn, matters were fast deteriorating, the thin line between life and death ever disintegrating.

A short news report in the British *Daily Herald* on November 1, 1938 stated,

'Nearly 4,000 Jews expelled from Germany on Friday and Saturday are still here waiting to be evacuated into the Polish interior or sent back to Germany. Altogether 6,000 people arrived, more than the entire population of the township, only 1,000 were able to leave on Sunday. The first arrivals by special train were unloaded before the surprised Polish officials had time to recover from the shock. Fearing that they would have difficulties with the following trainloads, the Germans emptied the train in German territory and drove the crowd across the fields into Poland. The worst plight was that of a transport of 150 refugees from Hamburg on Saturday morning. They were brought to Granski just north of Zbaszyn. I spoke to an elderly woman in that group. "As soon as we left the train," she said, "S.S. men, with fixed bayonets, ordered us to 'quick march'. It was cold and wet. The road was full of holes and traps. We were warned not to look back, but we heard machine guns being placed in position in our rear. 'We will fire,' they threatened us, 'if anyone tries to steal back.' Then suddenly there was a crack of rifle fire. People ran, fell down, and were beaten by the guards. Many were injured in the resulting stampede. We were pushed across a waterlogged ditch on the frontier into Polish territory.'"

The dire conditions these people had to endure were vividly described in this letter sent by one of the deportees to his family:

My Dear Ones,
You have probably already heard of my fate from Cilli. On October 27, Thursday evening at about 9 o'clock two men came from the crime police, demanded my passport, and then placed a deportation document

before me to sign and ordered me to accompany them immediately. Cilli and Bernard were already in bed. I had just finished my work and was sitting down to eat, but had to get dressed immediately and go with them. I was so upset I could scarcely speak a word. In all my life, I will never forget this moment. I was locked up in the Castle prison like a criminal. It was a bad night for me. On Friday at 4 o'clock in the afternoon we were taken to the main station under strict guard by police and S.S. where everybody was given two loaves of bread and margarine and then loaded onto the freight cars. It was a cruel picture of weeping women and children and heart-breaking scenes. We were then taken to the border in sealed cars under the strictest police guard.

When we reached the border at 5 o'clock on Saturday afternoon we were pushed across. A new terrible scene was revealed here. We spent three days on the platform and in the waiting rooms, 8,000 people. Women and children fainted, went mad, people died, faces as yellow as wax. It was like a cemetery full of dead people. I was also amongst those who fainted. There was nothing to eat except dry prison bread, without anything to drink. I never slept at all for two nights on the platform, where I collapsed. There was no room even to stand. The air was pestilential. Women and children were half-dead. On the fourth day help at last arrived, doctors, nurses with medicine, butter and bread from the Jewish Committee in Warsaw. Then we were taken to barracks where there was straw on the floor on which we could lie down...'

Was I really part of this expulsion? I have no recollection of these scenes. Or of the suffering, indignation and utter shock at what was happening. Of course, I was very young but to remember nothing? My mind has protected me from the horror by forcing me to forget. Maybe I should consider myself lucky to have managed to blank out these memories. And yet the knowledge of it all still troubles me nearly eighty years later.

The writing was on the wall, loud and clear, yet much of the world chose to ignore the signs and turn a blind eye. Has anything changed? There are those who still prefer to argue for an illusion of good in evil, and from their distant safe havens preach non-resistance and non-interference.

One of the few exceptions were the people of Britain. The barbaric acts of *Kristallnacht* and the atrocious treatment of those expelled obviously made an impression on all faiths and most political strands of the British public, to the point that a lengthy debate on 'Racial, Religious and Political Minorities' took place in parliament on November 21, 1938, just one month after the announcement of the Polish decree.

At 7.33 p.m. the member for Derby, Mr. Noel Baker, stood up to begin his speech:

'I beg to move that this house notes with profound concern the deplorable treatment suffered by certain racial, religious and political minorities in Europe, and in view of the growing gravity of the refugee problem, would welcome an immediate concerted effort amongst the nations, including the United States of America, to secure a common policy.'

He completed his speech forty-five minutes later... 'I hope they [the government] will now give permits for the ten thousand children whom the Jews are eager to welcome.'

Reader, they did.

And as a direct result I arrived, on August 29, 1939, at Cotton Wharf, on the banks of the Thames as part of what became known as the Kindertransport.

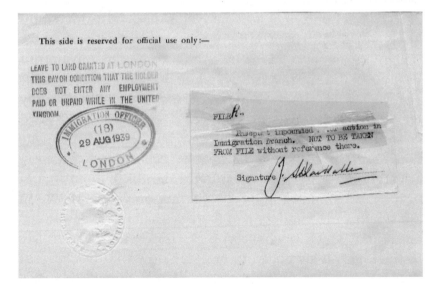

This document ... 36730 NAME: *Reich, Erich* ... s Majesty's Government in the United Kin... ... ...he United Kingdom for educational purposes ... ... Inter-Aid Committee for children.

THIS DOCUMENT REQUIRES NO VISA.

PERSONAL PARTICULARS.

Name REICH   ERICH

Sex   MALE   Date of Birth 30 - 4 - 35

Place WIEN

Full Names and Address of Parents

REICH   Schapse & Mina

ZBONSZYN

This side is reserved for official use only:—

LEAVE TO LAND GRANTED AT LONDON THIS DAY ON CONDITION THAT THE HOLDER DOES NOT ENTER ANY EMPLOYMENT PAID OR UNPAID WHILE IN THE UNITED KINGDOM

IMMIGRATION OFFICER
(18)
29 AUG 1939
LONDON

FILE...

Passport impounded . ... action in Immigration Branch.   NOT TO BE TAKEN FROM FILE without reference there.

Signature ...

The two sides of the British government document allowing me entry into the United Kingdom without a Visa

The Jewish community and many Christian groups including the Quakers had already agreed to underwrite the costs so that the children would not become a financial burden on the state. The United Kingdom made up of charming, ancient islands, often maddeningly arrogant and insular, frequently parochial and blinkered, opened its heart to thousands of refugee children and without a shadow of a doubt saved all our lives.

According to the weather forecast, 'A shallow depression over the Bay of Biscay was slowly spreading north, bringing with it bright intervals and local thunderstorms.' A very English reception, I have since learned. To my east, well out of sight, the Vienna Eye, the 'Reisenrad', in the shadows of which I was born. That same Ferris wheel on which Orson Welles had yet to make his famous speech in *The Third Man* talking of the dawn of the Italian Renaissance, which sprang from the murderous lifestyle of the Borgias family, while the sole heritage of 600 years of Swiss democracy was the cuckoo clock. To my west, just up the river, no inkling yet of the London Eye.

An inextricable link exists between them. Both elevate you to the scintillating heights of beauty and emotion. Together they also lower you to the depths of anguish and despair. Most importantly, depending on your outlook on life, you begin to understand there is a balance in emotional behaviour which I believe you can exert control over. My instinct has always been to not stay down in the dark for too long, but to get back up as quickly as possible because the scenery is much brighter, more enticing, uplifting and far-reaching when seen from above. Looking down from the pinnacle a sense of elevation and achievement begins to pervade, helping one to take a more positive outlook on life. Far better than remaining in a dark, depressing and self-made undergrowth, from which there appears to be no relief or light at the end of the tunnel.

There are times my mood can swing and I become melancholy, sad that I have no personal recollections of my very early childhood, of my parents and the close family who saw me develop from a baby into a toddler, take my first steps and utter some initial, stuttering words. A typical Jewish family environment which would have dreamt of my future as a doctor, lawyer, accountant, tailor, or even a rabbi.

The mind though does weird and wonderful things, and when too much turmoil invades the earlier part of your life it forms a protective shield. Unfortunately, though, it's not selective. Consequently, while I would dearly love to have some of the happy images of those early days, it's not possible without bringing into focus the dark and torrid elements of that period.

What did I feel in that moment, standing on the precipice of separation from the warmth of parental love and protection? Was I aware, even if only subconsciously, of the new life confronting me in a strange country with an incomprehensible language and rather peculiar cultural customs, where saying one thing might often mean something entirely different. Not dissimilar, I suppose, to the way some words are spelt in the English language. You write the word one way but pronounce it in another. Quite a lot to contend with at the tender age of four, separated from your entire immediate family.

Jacques, the eldest, had arrived in England on a sailing to London sometime in June 1939.

Ossie, the nearer to me in age, and I came together and it was Ossie who looked after me on our sea-journey to freedom. Once in England, Ossie was almost immediately evacuated from London with thousands of other children to Ely in Cambridgeshire under the auspices of the Jewish Free School which had been located in the East End of London. I've often wondered how the inhabitants of that beautiful East Anglian cathedral city reacted when confronted with not just a horde of unruly London children but a large number of non-English-speaking Jewish kids to boot. I can only surmise it must have caused considerable concern, confusion and even some emotional instability. After all, was this not the start of an irreversible continental influence over the English way of life?

Being too young to go to school, I was separated from Ossie.

I have made numerous phone calls, studied the committee meeting minutes of all the relevant London boroughs and scoured newspaper articles from the time, but am still no wiser about my movements after I stepped down from the ship, the *Warszawa*, that brought me to England on that warm, thundery day at the end of August 1939. I did, however, find a number of news reports about our arrival. Under the headline '70 Child Refugees Arrive', on August 30, 1939, the *Daily Mail* reported: 'Deported from Germany, and unable to return to their native Poland, 70 children who have been kept in a "No Man's Land" between the frontiers of the two countries for nearly a year, arrived in London yesterday on the Polish ship *Warszawa*.

They were met by Mr. George Lansbury M.P., chairman of the Polish Refugee Fund, which is responsible for bringing the young refugees to this country. The children will stay here till they are eighteen, but the three Polish officials who brought them over are returning.'

Another newspaper reported that one of the children had drawn a picture of the Mill and Field kitchen at Zbaszyn on a handkerchief, with the inscription: 'Learn to suffer and don't complain, sunshine always follows rain.'

All I now know is that some twelve months later I was in Burchett House, a refugee hostel in the delightful London commuter town of Dorking. Not being with me at this time, my brothers weren't able to tell me how I got there.

It was in fact due to the composer Ralph Vaughn Williams who brought out many Jewish musicians from central Europe. On one of his visits to the Jewish Centre at Bloomsbury House, he was told that there were some children they didn't know what to do with. His quick response was, 'I am the chairman of the Dorking Refugee Committee (which he had founded with amongst others E. M. Forster) and we have a refugee home where we can absorb them.'

And so my new life began.

Chapter Three

Dorking, aged 5-11

We wove a web in childhood
A web of sunny air
We dug a spring in infancy
Of water pure and fair
We sowed in youth a mustard seed
We cut an almond rod
We are now grown up to riper age
Are they withered in the sod?

Charlotte Brontë

My first real memory is the tiny room I slept in. I can still see the rather crumbled stone walls, on which I used to scratch primitive drawings during the long summer evenings when I couldn't sleep. Although small and cosy, the only way in and out was through my foster parents' bedroom, so once in my room it was hard to go out if they were in bed themselves. Imagine the difficulties that presented, particularly when I needed the loo, which even more inconveniently, was located at the far end of the public corridor.

One summer evening when they were out, having for safety locked my little bedroom door, the inevitable happened. I felt a desperate urge for the toilet. There was no way I was going to wet the bed so I opened the window, prayed nobody was in the garden below, and relieved myself. Even precariously balanced on a stool I could hardly reach above the windowsill to release the agonising pressure building up inside me. Despite not being able to sleep half the night – my mind filled with guilt pangs and worrying that I might have been seen or, worse still, that I might have hit somebody – the incident was never mentioned.

My foster parents, Joseph and Emilie Kreibich, or mutti and fater as I called them, were pretty strict but to me quite wonderful. By making me part of their family, I believe they gave me a sense of belonging, of being loved and wanted, of providing that warm safety net we yearn for during the awkward growing up period, so full of doubts and anxieties. As a consequence, I believe I retained a semblance of emotional stability, which otherwise could so easily have been lost amidst the trauma of the early separation from my parents.

Joseph and Emilie were also refugees — Christian socialists from Sudetenland, the German-speaking part of Czechoslovakia — who, like me, had fled from the Nazis. Of the dozen or so refugee families living in Burchett House, they were the only ones who weren't Jewish yet it was the Kreibichs, already grandparents, who fostered me. It couldn't have been an easy decision for them. I was, apparently, a rather unhealthy, scrawny, spotty-skinned specimen. None of us could speak English, our common language being German. I was young so I overcame the language barrier and learnt English at school. My foster parents never did. On the other hand, having no option but to communicate with them in German, I can still hold a reasonable conversation in the language, albeit not always too coherently and frequently using rather childish words.

After time, I must have felt part of their family as it never occurred to me that they weren't my real parents. Deep down inside I must have realised that I wasn't their son, after all their name was Kreibich, mine was Reich. Nevertheless, the possibility of originating from a different background, with parents living in another country – siblings, aunts and uncles all with a culture alien to the one I was being brought up in – never entered my mind. Patently, nature had come to the rescue and allowed me to obliterate what had gone on before. In any event, at the age of five it would have been too complicated, and probably unbearable, to even contemplate such a possibility.

My world was now the Kreibich family: their children Emma and Rudl, and their grandchildren Emily, Rudy and Sonya – who was a couple of years younger than myself – and baby Ida. I was included in all their outings, whether blueberry-picking on the damp slopes of Leith Hill, mushroom-collecting in the nearby Glory Woods, or visiting their Sudetenland cronies dotted all around the region. I'm hardly likely to forget the time we set out late one autumn afternoon to collect walnuts. Not finding many on the ground, or within easy reach, I decided to throw large stones into the trees hoping to bring down a shower of nuts. What I actually hit was a hornets' nest, attracting their direct attention and wrath, and instigating my own flight of the bumble bees. Seven stings later I made the first of several visits to the local Cottage Hospital.

During the first few years as part of the Kreibich family I attended Sunday school, becoming a regular visitor at St Paul's Church, where I went with my foster parents.

Aside from the normal humdrum daily routine, there are several incidents that stand out. As I described in the previous chapter the most important was the arrival of my brother Jacques. It was the first time I was confronted with the fact that I wasn't the person I'd thought I was. It forced me to face the reality that the Kreibichs were not my parents. While my relationship with them never changed, inevitably, many aspects of life altered quite dramatically as a consequence of Jacques' visit.

For a start, no more going to church, which I probably didn't really miss that much, even though I enjoyed the lovely melodic hymns and Christmas carols. Sunday school stories from the Bible could be quite absorbing for a young mind trying to work out how, for example, it was possible to feed a crowd of five thousand with so few fish – a feat I've still to solve, despite having several times visited the very spot this miracle is supposed to have taken place, on the shores of the Sea of Galilee.

Christmas celebrations didn't change either, thankfully. Engrained in my mind is the memory of a tiny fir tree there each year, adorned with an abundance of hanging silver strips and one lonely, carefully selected present waiting to be unwrapped. Once it turned out to be Joseph's handmade Meccano set; another, a tiny clockwork train running up and down a single track, just two feet long. I had hours of unalloyed fun playing with these magical toys. Christmas would not have been the same without the constant sound of carols pouring out over the radio waves and every now and again Emilie exclaiming, 'Erich, ruhe bitte!' *Erich, quiet please!* when either *Stille Nacht* or *O Tannenbaum* filled the room. 'Aren't these just beautiful carols?' she would repeat, over and over again.

Even now, come mid-November when the carols herald the long odyssey towards Christmas, the first few notes of *Silent Night* instantly conjure up the image of Emilie; short and round, her grey hair sharply brushed back over her head. One couldn't help but be attracted to her soft blue-green eyes and delightful, warm, oval face. Somehow, she always seemed to be wearing an apron and was forever busy, cleaning, cooking, making jam or curdled cheese, which stank to high heaven. Emilie was a proper, down-to-earth 'Yiddishe momma' who wasn't Jewish. I must confess I found these moments pure joy. They were occasions to savour, when all seemed at peace. Goodwill pervaded the atmosphere and became the focus of our lives. Occasionally, I was allowed a sip of sweet homemade blueberry wine, filling me with pride at being considered grown up enough to taste this very mildly alcoholic drink. Maybe they just pretended it was wine, and not juice, to make me feel good. Either way it worked.

But no more going to church meant instead starting Hebrew classes with the rabbi in Dorking. The whole culture of Rabbi Kohn's house – the food, the small talk and the smells – might have come from outer space as far as I was concerned. I never got used to that environment, and never really connected with the rabbi's children with whom I later went to school. The world I was born into had, in a matter of a few short years, become entirely alien to me. I did eventually slowly return to its outer fringes but on a somewhat different premise, one based on heritage rather than religion.

There are times when my mind wanders back to that period. I wonder how, after only five or six years, two brothers, brought up together from babyhood were unable to recognise each other. It really is quite frightening. It seems that human nature, in order to help build a new and stable existence, is quite capable of overcoming hardships by blocking out virtually all the experiences of the past – good and bad. Whilst it's essential to understand and learn from the past, constantly living in its shadow won't necessarily create a brighter future.

What also remained stable during that period were my periodic visits to Vaughn Williams's house. These were not the most entertaining afternoons I've spent. How was I to know the honour bestowed on me, meeting and having tea with one of Britain's most eminent composers. He must have thought I had some musical ability, as he sent me to an elderly teacher to find out whether I should have piano lessons. Imagine the blow to my self-esteem, which was pretty low at the best of times, on being told, in so many words, that I was tone deaf.

I have deluded myself ever since that this must have been a rather rash and hasty conclusion, by what appeared to me a rather cold-hearted old woman who probably wasn't much over forty. To this day I can't play a musical instrument, but nothing gives me greater pleasure than listening to music – whether at home, while driving, or in the concert halls. Anyway, I got my own back; nearly all my children found themselves having to study at least one musical instrument whether they liked it or not. Mostly they did.

I found out more about my life from the minutes of the meetings of the Dorking Refugee Committee meetings often chaired by Vaughn Williams himself. The majority of these minutes have survived and all have a section on children, where my name keeps cropping up. 'Erich is unhappy at school; he has skin problems and requires infra-red treatment. Erich needs new shoes, he should be given a shilling a week pocket money,' and so on. 'Mrs Hardisty, from the Jewish Refugee Committee, wants Erich removed to a Jewish children's home so that he can receive Jewish religious education. Miss Evans from the Dorking Refugee Committee believes that this would be detrimental to Erich's wellbeing, seeing that he is happy with the Kreibichs and doing well at school.'

At the time, of course, I had no idea of what was going on in the background; of the continual battle between giving me a religious education and keeping me stable in the caring environment of a family. Fortunately, the Dorking Refugee Committee held sway until after my thirteenth birthday. I shudder to think how I would have handled a move to a children's home at the age of eight or nine. Who knows if my mind could have blocked out any more traumatic experiences.

The minutes also reminded me what it was like during those dark, rather frightening days of the Second World War. Many of the committee's members were ordinary local citizens, born and bred in Dorking, most of whose English ancestry stretched back many generations. One can't help but marvel at their generosity in taking up the cause of refugees with whom, up until then, they had very little in common, both culturally and linguistically. On top of which, most of these refugees came from the enemy country and could only converse in German. Delving into the minutes, it's quite clear that the members' main priority was the wellbeing of the children.

More recently I was contacted by a gentleman who, it turns out, was evacuated as a six-year-old to Dorking and sat next to me at St Martin's Primary School. I couldn't remember him so I enquired how he managed to recall not only me but my name as well. He explained, 'You looked so sad, miserable, and rather unhealthy, on top of which you couldn't speak or understand English. We used to go out into the playground together and I shared my Horlicks tablets with you. You've even remained part of my family folklore ever since. I often relate the story of the sad little boy I sat next to during my own traumatic experience at the beginning of the war as an evacuated child.'

It just proves you can never tell how each of us is affected by similar circumstances. One day I might find some Horlicks tablets and discover if their taste brings back any memories.

Between the ages of ten and thirteen, and periodically throughout my life, I have the distinct impression of myself colliding with and being buffeted by unforeseen incidents which have steered and deflected me involuntarily each time from one maelstrom into a still more complicated situation. These events and experiences also appear to have left indelible marks on the very core of my being, influencing subsequent actions I took, and shaping the human individual that I've become. There were, of course, the usual scrapes I managed to get myself entangled in. Such as pouring a bucket of boiling water over my leg and being one of the first to have penicillin cream smeared over the burn by a 'Sudeten' doctor family friend, who happened to be around at the time. Whether it actually helped I couldn't say, but I do remember I was in pain for several days after that accident.

I also managed to find myself in the isolation ward of a hospital located in the nearby village of Westcott for a serious case of the measles. Unfortunately, because of the strict visiting rules of the time, my foster mother couldn't come and see me as frequently as she or I would have liked, which for a seven-year-old was somewhat disheartening.

Then there was the case of waking up in a cold sweat because, in a nightmare, I couldn't get away from the Wicked Witch of the East after having pleaded to be taken, as a special treat, to see *The Wizard of Oz* the previous day. In my dream, the escapade took place in the large back garden of Burchett House, in the middle of which stood a majestic and beautiful chestnut tree. The problem was, I was desperately trying to reach the tree, in order to climb to safety, but never seemed to be getting any nearer. It was, I believe, my imaginary aching leg muscles that finally woke me up.

There are few dreams I remember as vividly as that one.

Chapter Four

Dorking and London, aged 11-13

How beautiful is youth that is always slipping away
Whoever wants to be happy, let him be so,
Of tomorrow there is no knowing.

Lorenzo de Medici

One spring day, just after my eleventh birthday, a serious incident occurred. Emilie and Joseph must have been under the illusion that, having commenced my second decade on earth relatively unscathed, I was to be trusted. What a misconception that turned out to be.

I was asked to take a package to some friends living on the other side of town. The parcel was heavy and cumbersome so it was agreed that I could use their handcart. Sonia, their eldest grandchild, pleaded to come with me and be pulled along in the cart. The negotiations successfully completed, I was sworn not to ride in the cart. I have since learned that the word 'promise' means something quite different to children than it does to parents. For offspring, it's simply a way of getting what you want by uttering its magic formula. For parents, it's a method of trying to keep their children out of harm's way. Neither can claim much success.

Anyway, very excited, off we went. The next thing I remember was waking up in the Cottage Hospital. Apparently, not only hadn't I kept my promise but on reaching the top of the hill, just past St Paul's Church, I'd decided it would be much more fun to get into the cart in front of Sonia and hurtle down, across a main road and straight into a wall. The outcome: a reconstructed nose, four weeks in hospital and a lengthy, detailed lecture in both German and English about what an irresponsible, stupid boy I was and how lucky both Sonia and I were to be alive.

Despite my being severely admonished, my foster parents' love for me never wavered. Not surprisingly, the accident had a rather more lasting effect on me. I have a tendency to snore, find it difficult to get rid of a cold once contracted, have an inclination towards vertigo – which appears to be becoming more pronounced with age – and, horror of horrors, I can't scuba dive nor have ever been able to make it into the skiing fraternity, as a result of the incident's effect on my balance.

My first reaction, on waking up some forty-eight hours after the crash, was to ask whether I had had my tonsils out. It was, at the time, the fashionable thing to do; a cure for all colds, coughs and the flu. A mirror held up by one of the nurses quickly dispelled that notion. Once it had been made clear what had brought me to the hospital, and I was able to absorb the utter stupidity of my action, matters improved dramatically. For a start, I was one of the youngest patients so the nurses made a fuss of me, which, of course, raised my morale no end. More importantly, the hospital building lay adjacent to the side garden of Burchett House. When I was allowed to get out of bed, a week or so later, I looked straight onto the rather unkempt lawn, which under normal circumstances served as my playground.

Instead of only being able to see me during the strict visiting hours, I could chat with my foster parents from the balcony. On one of these occasions Emilie waved a white envelope in great excitement. I had passed the eleven-plus. To be honest, that slice of stress had quite slipped my mind. They were so proud, so happy, and I felt that perhaps I had given them something back, and redeemed myself for all the anxious moments I'd caused them. It turned out I was one of the very few pupils from St Martin's Primary School to pass the exam. I can't work out how I managed this particular feat, as a non-native who, a few years earlier, wasn't actually aware that a country called England even existed.

There are times one wonders why it's necessary to radically overhaul systems that, by and large, appear to be working. Often, it seems, the only reason is that there are politicians who have a burning desire to make their mark on society by persuading us that the present, good or bad, is history, old-fashioned and consequently must be drastically altered, even if the current system is proving relatively effective. A good example was the view that grammar schools were elitist, a sort of upper class evil from the past to be eradicated at all costs. It was a bit like throwing the baby out with the bath water, and forgetting in the process that it gave a lot of children, like me, the chance for a more academic education. After all I couldn't exactly be typified as a product of the English middle class. Neither my foster parents nor I were particularly fluent in the English language, and they certainly weren't able to help tutor me towards passing exams.

Be that as it may, I had a tremendous sense of pride in passing the eleven-plus, and later enjoyed wearing my Dorking Grammar School uniform which the Dorking Refugee Committee paid for.

I loved the solitary daily walks to and from school, even if it did take nearly an hour meandering each way.

Dorking Grammar School opened up a new and wider vista. The sheer size and number of children sent shock waves through me. The buildings and playing fields were to me vast. How would I possibly survive in such surroundings? I, one of the only boys from that tiny St Martin's Primary School, where we were lucky to have had a playground, never mind playing fields. Excitement was quickly followed by apprehension once we were made fully conversant with the rules and regulations, the majority being restrictions – all about what one is not allowed to do and, of course, the consequences. Little mention of privileges; these had to wait until the sixth form. That is, if you managed to survive until then.

The problem was that being so busy absorbing the surroundings I didn't really take on board most of this tedious information. As a result, I was forced to learn by experience. During the two years I spent at the school I managed to find myself outside the headmaster Mr Jones's office on at least three separate occasions – for the sole purpose of receiving the cane for talking in the dinner queue, or similar misdemeanours. Twice, I was hauled up in front of obnoxious sixth form prefects. The first time was for running into school through the 'holy' front door, which we'd been specifically warned was not allowed, and the second for not wearing my tie properly and, even worse, for forgetting my school cap altogether. The latter is a sin both at school and according to my religion. I consoled myself that neither God nor the rabbi ever physically admonished me for that particular irregularity.

Anyway, if any of those prefects are still around, they will no doubt be pleased to learn that nearly seventy years later I still never wear a hat, and rarely a tie. Furthermore, I have still to discover the educational significance, or value, of allowing older pupils to use the main door while the younger ones were obliged to enter through the 'tradesmen's entrance'.

I wasn't a bad pupil, not near the top of the class but above average, and I rarely shirked homework. Despite several 'friendly' visits to the headmaster, I suppose I could be regarded as one of those pupils who didn't cause the teachers serious concerns. I did however make a small mark on the athletic field. For reasons best known to the school, every February, in the middle of winter – come rain, wind or snow – we had to take part in the cross-country race.

During the run in my first year, one of my trainers got stuck in the mud. I pulled it out, and with one trainer in my hand and the other on my foot, finished the race somewhere around twentieth place. Plenty of giggles and outright laughter accompanied me to the final stretch and beyond. I had stood out, made an impression, but not quite in the way I would have wished. On the positive side, I didn't give up, with or without shoes.

The following year, remembering the previous debacle, I made a point of tying my shoelaces properly. This time however, I hadn't paid much attention to the route instructions which, because of the atrocious weather conditions, had been altered. How was I to know that at a junction somewhere towards the end of the race I would find myself in front of everybody and therefore with no-one to follow? I promptly took the wrong turning. Fortuitously, one of the masters noticed and shouted for me to come back. Despite the extra yards I'd had to cover I still somehow managed to win the race, much to the surprise of all and sundry, including myself.

With my cross-country cup

Needless to say, Emilie and Joseph were delighted and so proud but then, quite unashamedly, so was I. Pictures galore were taken of me holding the cup. It turned out that I had apparently won the race just seven seconds outside the school record. If only I had concentrated when the detailed directions were given my name might have appeared for posterity in the school's annals; anyway, that's what I tell myself.

Long distant running has slipped in and out of my life, the loneliness of the long-distance runner suited my personal temperament. Moments, sometimes hours, to reflect on what has been going on in my life – trying to make sense of where I was heading and, above all, a time to daydream and consider how to overcome the many emotional events crowding in on me.

The problem is that, after running about half an hour or so, you become more aware of and concerned about your aching legs and bursting lungs. Your mind then begins to focus on the mundane issue of surviving to the end of the run. It's only after you finish, and while happily singing under a hot shower wondering how you made it, your mind suddenly switches back and, like waking up after a good night's sleep, what appeared an unbearable burden the night before has miraculously disappeared and become a solvable issue.

At around this time bad news and death caught up with me again.

I feel I have been dogged with losing people close to me, disappearing at crucial times in my life, all taking their toll on me in one way or another. My foster father, unbeknown to me, was suffering from angina pectoris. The day he died, at the age of fifty-five, remains engraved in my mind. Earlier in the day, I was so excited to be chosen as a reserve for the junior second-eleven soccer team. The trouble was, having only been informed during the afternoon break, there was no way I could either tell, or get permission from, my foster parents. Phones were not in abundance in the 1940s, let alone such unimagined innovations as mobiles. So, I made my own decision and stayed on after school. Unfortunately, nobody broke a limb and the school was winning so no substitute was needed and I didn't play.

I arrived home in the dark, two hours later than usual. A stern, worried-faced Emilie sent me down to the workshop where Joseph was repairing some chairs. All hell broke loose. The same anger and words most worried parents use when their offspring aren't home at the time they should be were heaped on me. Straight to bed without supper – no amount of pleading, apologies or histrionics helped.

I woke up in the middle of the night to the sound of a considerable commotion emanating from my foster parents' room. Peeping through, I could make out several people, including our doctor, hovering over the bed. Noticing me, Emilie came to the door where I was standing. 'Vater ist gerade gestorben,' *Father has just died,* she whispered while hugging me. Even as I write, goose pimples creep over my skin. It was so unexpected, such a sudden bolt out of the blue. Yes, he had been pretty strict, but he always found time to talk to me. He never made me feel anything but part of the family.

I carry his image with me – that stern face with the small, trimmed moustache, the typical worker's cap tightly drawn over his head, and his entire frame covered with sawdust.

We used to sit side by side for hours, building some construction or other with the Meccano set he'd made for me. He'd patiently try and explain how best to use the tools. Unfortunately, my hands being rather clumsy, most of the finished products were his creations rather than mine. I admired and loved him and felt completely safe in his company; emotions I always felt were reciprocated.

The next few days were traumatic. He lay on his bed for several days before the funeral; which meant I was obliged to pass the body each time I entered or left my room. This, of course, heightened my sense of guilt. For a long time, I was sure the row we'd had, caused the stroke and that his death was somehow my fault. The sickening, sweet smell that accompanied his lying in-state has remained embedded in my sensory memory bank.

The funeral took place in the cemetery just outside Dorking on one of those typical dreary, grey, late-autumn days. We were all in tears; heads bowed, each with his or her individual thoughts and grief. As the coffin was lowered into the ground I recalled many of the moments we had shared; like walking up Leith Hill, picking blueberries to make Christmas wine.

A CZECH SOCIALIST: DEATH IN DORKING OF JOSEF KREIBICH.

Mr. Josef Kreibich, a prominent figure in the Socialist movement of Czechoslovakia, died at Burchett House, the Dorking Refugee Hostel, on Tuesday, August 26th, at the age of 55. He had been one of the founders of the Czechoslovak Socialist Workers' Movement, and played an important part in the Trade Unions, the Co-operative Society, and the Workers' Republican Defence Organisation. After the German occupation of Czechoslovakia, Mr. Kreibich, a Sudeten German by birth, fled to France with a Socialist Group of Czech Sudeten Germans; and five months later, in August, 1939, the whole group came to England. A large part of the group emigrated together to form a Settlement in Canada, but Mr. Kreibich remained in England, with the purpose of returning to his beloved homeland as soon as possible, to help in its reconstruction. This hope was never fulfilled, although Mr. Kreibich lived to see the defeat of the Germans, because of the understandable but cruel attitude of the Czech Government towards all Czechs of German origin, whatever their political opinions.

During the past eight years, Mr. Kreibich had become a familiar figure in Dorking. Although his poor health prevented him from taking a permanent job, he was never idle; he was for many years the leader of the Refugee Hostel in Dorking, and he and his wife showed the truth of their ideals by taking a small orphan refugee boy into their family.

The funeral took place at Dorking Cemetery on Friday last, and was attended by several Czech and Sudeten friends, by members of the Dorking Refugee Committee, and by residents from the Hostel. Mr. de Witte, a Social Democrat, gave a memorial address, in which he spoke of the great work that Mr. Kreibich had done for the cause of freedom in Sudetenland, from 1919 until his forced escape in 1939.

Mr. Kreibich will be missed by many in Dorking.

The obituary for Josef Kreibich in the Dorking Advertiser August 1947

Being a carpentry craftsman, Joseph tried many times to help me create something in wood, but rather unsuccessfully, I'm afraid. Woodwork was the only subject at school in which I consistently failed and managed to finish bottom of the class. I thought of the small clockwork train that he and Emilie had given me the previous Christmas. Joseph gave me lengthy explanations as to how it all worked. I loved this little train, winding it up for hours on end until everybody became thoroughly sick and tired of its monotonous humming sound. I thought about the many absorbing evenings we'd spent together building some fairly odd-looking structures with the Meccano. Emilie and Joseph played rummy virtually every night. As a treat, I was allowed to join in at weekends, rarely winning but when I did what a fuss; it might as well have been an Olympic gold medal.

During the entire period of the war the radio was always on, blaring out intermittent news bulletins which I frequently had to translate. Every evening a different battle; losses and gains, numbers of soldiers killed or wounded and, at the end of all the news items, a reminder of the blackout. There was no getting away from the war. I can't begin to count the number of times we rushed down into the cellar when the sirens began their ominous wailing. Toward the end of the war, these shelter visits included counting to twenty-one and hoping the Doodlebug wouldn't land anywhere near us. As time went on we all appeared to have our designated spaces. For some reason only whispers could ever be heard. Nobody shouted, talked loudly or thought of singing. It was as if there was a belief that the bombs could seek us out by sound waves.

I suppose at the heart of this silence was the fear of what might lie ahead in the future. Joseph was always the one who led the way; the last to enter and the first to ensure that it was safe to leave, often well after the 'all clear' had sounded.

The war years left many scattered images. Some became indelible impressions that have remained part of my psyche.

About fifteen years ago I visited Churchill's War Rooms, near Whitehall. As you enter the dark, narrow passage a siren starts wailing. It stopped me in my tracks and, as if in a time warp, I was transported back seventy-plus years. A time filled with blackouts, running with schoolmates to and from the shelters, Doodlebugs flying overhead, and many other war-related incidents, instantly flashed through my mind.

Being young children, fear never seemed an issue, nor did we understand the destruction and huge loss of life that accompanies war. At times, it was all rather exciting, like an adventure that has no set rules or ending. Double summer time, and air raids happening in the evening, allowed us to stay up all hours of the night. And why should we care if an air raid occurred during school hours, disrupting lessons? Running to the shelters proved far more interesting than learning one's times table, off by heart. Frankly, it's a wonder we learned anything. On the other hand, in the process of trying to make sense of what the war was really all about, we grew up pretty fast. Given that there was no television to show the horrors, it meant that when we listened to the news, or read the papers, it was our imaginations that were expanded, not the reality.

On my way to and from school I used to pass a large walled house where American soldiers were billeted during the latter half of the war. Being rather nosy, I would frequently peep through the fence or climb up a tree on the other side of the road. It was a pretty pointless exercise as the G.I.s were rarely visible outside the building. One afternoon, though, a soldier wandering inside the compound waved and told me to wait a moment, then disappeared into the house. A few minutes later he returned with a long curved yellow 'thing' in his hand and asked whether I had ever eaten what he was holding. The fact is I didn't have a clue what it was, never mind having eaten one.

'This is a banana,' he laughingly explained. 'You can have it,' he went on,' but if you eat too many all at once you could die.' It took me years to muster up the courage and swallow more than one banana a week, even when they became plentiful.

The merry-making on V.E. day was something to behold. The entire population of Dorking seemed to be out on the streets; everyone dancing, singing and basically making as much noise as possible. It was as if a dam had burst, allowing never-ending gushes of water to cascade unhindered and unabated. We all hugged each other. Well, the adults did. We youngsters were somewhat more circumspect, but then we didn't really understand the significance of this sudden mayhem. Most extraordinarily, as daylight turned into dusk, and darkness descended, fireworks flared into the night sky. The streetlights were switched on and we just stood and gaped.

With my foster mum

In retrospect, saddest for me was that neither then, whilst celebrating the end of the war, or at any time before, did it enter my mind that amongst the casualties of that ghastly war were my parents, and many of my close family. Nor was I able, as a mere ten-year-old, to stand back and grasp that this war had, in fact, turned my life upside down.

I had been living with the Kreibichs over six years when my foster father died in 1947 and I can honestly say that it was a period during which I felt most safe and secure. But from the moment Joseph died, life changed. The pressure to remove me from Burchett House, so that I could get a better Jewish education, intensified. The fact that I was receiving a very good education at a highly respected grammar school, without any help from well-meaning strangers, didn't seem to matter. Nor did it occur to those well-meaning people so worried about my religious education that having been well brought up – lovingly cared for and happy – was reason enough to leave well alone. Everybody thought they knew what was best for me, even though none of them had been physically part of my life during those crucial years of constant upheaval, turmoil and growing up.

In order for me to be exposed to my Jewish religious heritage, the Jewish Refugee Committee in London arranged for me to spend Pesach with the Sachs Family in Golders Green (Mrs Sachs was herself a *Kind*, one of those who had also come across on the Kindertransport). Standing in synagogue for what seemed an interminable amount of time, trying to fathom out a constant stream of unintelligible, mumbled words, was definitely a discovery but of the boring variety. And while I loved, and still do, the food served on the Seder night – chicken soup with dumplings, matzoth and all – telling the story of the Hagaddah turned out to be a never-ending saga. Any Rabbi that ever lived appears to have had a different interpretation of the Exodus; not only of the same story but also of identical sentences. Imagine, you ask four simple questions and you get three hours of convoluted answers, at the end of which you're still none the wiser. I now felt an outsider in both camps. It seemed a bit like how the onset of a possible schizophrenic episode might feel; finding yourself in limbo, not belonging anywhere but being part of everywhere at the same time.

And there was my real family too. My mother's brother Uncle Izzi and his wife Rose lived in London and had no children. They didn't offer to take me in even though I was Izzi's nephew and they must have known full well that the chances of ever seeing my parents again were pretty negligible. They let total strangers, with a very different culture and background, take on the responsibility of my upbringing. I presume they had their reasons but I never knew what they were.

I did see Uncle Izzi quite a few times and liked him very much. He was a storyteller, often entertaining me during our London escapades. I never truly knew when to believe him. According to Izzi, in his youth he'd been an outstanding athlete. Why, he'd even played table tennis for Vienna! That actually turned out to be the Viennese Jewish club, Hakoach Vienna. I can however, vouch for his 'dodging' abilities. On one of my visits in early 1948, just after a long, tedious Sabbath service session in synagogue, Izzi invited me to a football game. A wonderful antidote,

Chelsea playing Wolves at Stamford Bridge – an offer a twelve-year-old just couldn't refuse. It was my first real football match and I learned a few things that day.

As we approached the turnstiles, hemmed in from all sides by the crowds, Izzi suddenly turned around, bent down and whispered, 'Erich, don't say a word, just copy me.' I watched carefully. As he passed the ticket collector's window he pointed his right thumb back towards me and continued straight on. What could I do? Forward I trotted, and passed the window with thumb raised, feet quaking in my shoes. I really shouldn't have worried. Izzi relied on my being so short the ticket collector wouldn't notice my head let alone the thumb. He was of course right. We both got in without paying. Unfortunately, I've never been able to repeat that trick.

The sheer noise that hit us as we entered the stadium was exhilarating magic to me. That initial shock wave of sound, and its impact, was the highlight of the entire afternoon, certainly the most memorable moment. What a contrast to the morning's synagogue experience. One minute I'm in the company of people lost in prayer to and adulation of an unknown deity, the next I'm a tiny figure in a crowd letting out their emotions to real, live heroes on the pitch.

Although I really did enjoy the game, I can't actually remember what the score was or even who won. My feelings of guilt at not paying must have weighed heavily on me, otherwise how does one explain that since then, and to this very day, my entire family and I support Arsenal not Chelsea?

Undoubtedly, the *coup d'éclat* in Uncle Izzi's storytelling came from an entirely different part of his life. Around the time when plans were afoot for me to leave England and live in Israel, the film *The Third Man* was in the cinema. I went to see it, in the company of Uncle Izzi. As it happens, even apart from the haunting zither music which became a huge hit, I've always considered the film to be one of the greatest.

On our way out, Izzi asked, 'So, Erich — did you like it?'

'Very much,' I replied, quite truthfully.

'Do you remember the scene where the cat crawls over Harry Lime's shoes?' Uncle Izzi continued.

'How could I forget?'

'Well,' he responded. 'That's not Orson Welles, standing in the shadow of the door, that's me.'

What was I supposed to say to that? He must have seen the expression of incredulity on my face. He quickly continued, 'Didn't you know I was Orson Welles' stand-in?'

I most certainly didn't, although to be truthful Izzi's build was not dissimilar to that of the great actor/director. I've scoured every book I've ever been able to find about the film and its making. While I've discovered many fascinating details about Orson Welles, Graham Greene, Carol Reed and everybody else involved, Izzi's name – he was known as Ivor Spencer since coming to the UK – doesn't appear anywhere. One of those mysteries I'll never resolve, but will continue to enjoy believing.

With my brothers Jacques (Left) and Ossie (right) and our Uncle Izzy

The previous year I met my mother's only sister, Auntie Irene, for the first time. She was the youngest of the six siblings, my mother having been the eldest. Living in Israel with her husband, Dolphie, since before the war, she had come to England to see us all. She came to pick me up from Dorking and certainly had no problems communicating with Emilie, German being their mutual language as Irene had grown up in Vienna. A lot of firsts occurred during that visit. Travelling in a taxi, staying at the Cumberland Hotel in London, then considered a pretty posh establishment, accompanying a beautiful woman whose very presence turned men's heads as she walked by. To top it all she took me to the Odeon Marble Arch to see *The Magic Bow*. It left me an ardent admirer of Paganini, even though its star,

Stewart Granger, couldn't quite achieve the same dizzying artistic heights as the man himself. Yehudi Menuhin, who actually played the violin behind the scenes, was a different proposition altogether.

I was very taken with Auntie. She visited several times.

But in the background, pressure was mounting for me to leave Dorking and the only life I had ever really known. The combination of my foster father's death, my foster mother's deteriorating health, the Jewish community's strong desire for me to be in a more Jewish environment, and me being older and able to comprehend a little that I had a heritage all combined to become a strong force.

Thinking back, I feel I was brainwashed into leaving Dorking for the bright lights of London. But the delights of London I was ushered into turned out to be the ultra-religious Hasmonean School. Even for a hardened traveller like me, someone used to frequent changes in lifestyle, this proved one bridge too far. I lasted just three months, boarding with a group of boys whose main preoccupations appeared to be praying and trying to interpret the words of the Bible. Mind you, I couldn't have been in nicer surroundings. The house we were boarded in was located beside Hampstead Heath in the Vale of Health.

I also had a Bar Mitzvah, again through the good auspices of the Sachs family. At the time, I should have been pre-warned about my Bar Mitzvah. Being one of the few thirteen-year-old Jewish boys unable to read a portion of the Torah, I was only allowed to recite the prayers. Luckily, I somehow managed to learn these off by heart. Rather ironic, as only a few years later I could understand

and read Hebrew fluently; the same can't be said for many of those praying in synagogue.

The religious environment at the Hasmonean School was too much for me. Auntie had suggested that I come to live in Israel with them. I caved in and agreed to go. Her visit the previous summer had undoubtedly influenced me and helped make up my mind. The idea of going to live with somebody who actually wanted to look after me was very appealing. Not to mention her wonderful Ingrid Bergman look-alike features.

With Auntie and Ossie (right)

I had now attained the venerable age of thirteen-and-a-half. I was making life-changing decisions. Before setting off, there was the small matter of training for, and learning about the country I was immigrating to. I spent two weeks at a kind of training farm, near Thaxted in Essex, and learned that digging sugar beets with my bare hands out of frozen soil in the middle of winter isn't fun. These short weeks of hard work in icy conditions didn't prepare me at all for the heat or way of life I later encountered in Israel. It did, however, make me homesick and reminded me how happy I'd been in Dorking, the only place I could, at that time, truly call 'home'. Why, oh why, was I made to move?

As I'm writing, it's suddenly sunk in that during this period I never made any close friends. In fact, I'd become a bit of a loner. Whilst my character has evolved and become a little more outgoing, as someone who'd had to learn to be as happy in his own company as in the midst of a set of friends or siblings, underneath I can't say I've really changed that much.

I was on the move again.

Chapter Five

Aliyah, aged 13

Wandering between two worlds, one dead,
The other powerless to be born,
With nowhere yet to rest my head,
Like these, on earth I wait forlorn.

Mathew Arnold

My journey to Israel turned out rather quirky; a sort of *Young Person's Guide to Travel Escapades on Earth*. Yet again, I was on the move to a destination I didn't know, in the company of people I'd never met before and was unlikely to meet again. And, once more, I was one of the youngest. Looking back, I feel that these frequent moves at such a young age must have caused much of the restlessness that seems to have imbued my character, shaped my personality, and dogged me throughout my adult life. Although at the time it was also an exciting adventure, an unknown mystery to look forward to.

We were a group of about a dozen youngsters between the ages of thirteen and eighteen on our way to the Promised Land, to meet up with near relatives and experience a new way of life. Most of us had lost our immediate families in the Holocaust and were travelling with high expectations of a home, family and a safe haven where we could start life afresh.

I had absolutely no idea what to expect. I simply assumed – and fervently hoped – that I would find this life less rigorously religious than the one I had encountered at the Hasmonean School. Anyway, the thought of being cared for by Auntie Irene, my mother's beautiful and sophisticated younger sister, was undoubtedly an added bonus.

I don't remember much about the journey to Marseilles, except that it was pretty tedious and took considerably longer than I had anticipated. We seemed to spend an inordinate amount of time on platforms, changing and waiting for trains. The week spent in Marseilles, though, was a different proposition. While the details of the daily routine have escaped me, some of the more dubious activities we became involved with have remained in my memory.

Our accommodation, pretty basic but no worse than the standards I was familiar with, was located on a hill overlooking the harbour. Even in the middle of winter, to our young, naive eyes the panoramic views of the sea were uplifting; beauty encapsulated. Crucially, we were let loose every day for several hours. Enough time to be taught by the older members of the group how to choke on strong French cigarettes, consume alcohol and basically behave a bit like fully fledged juvenile delinquents. We didn't really get into trouble; it was just a swiftly taken opportunity to unburden and forget the traumas of the still very recent and raw past. I was careful not to impart these particular details to my offspring until well after they were into their late teens. Not because I was embarrassed, but to ensure they weren't provided with an excuse to follow in my footsteps like, 'You were smoking and drinking at thirteen, so, why can't I?'

I am full of wonder at the parallels that can occur in life. We boarded the *Eilat*, a small passenger freight ship, not dissimilar to the *Warszawa* that had brought me to England a decade earlier. Both were of a similar size, both had passed their 'sell by date' and, more significantly, neither lasted long after these sailings. The *Warszawa* was torpedoed during the war, somewhere off the coast of Africa. The *Eilat* was sent to the scrap yard soon after our arrival in Israel. While I have no recollection of the former, the latter would be difficult to forget.

On boarding the ship, we were met with a hearty 'Shalom', *Peace*, a greeting used in a variety of forms by many cultures. Do we really understand the meaning of the word, or is it simply a concept we find easier and more comfortable to express than put into practice?

The food, our first culture shock, included strange new things such as humus and tahini made from chickpeas and sesame seeds. They went down pretty well, even though they were rudely slapped on to our tin plates. Early preparation for the army. The slabs of sweet halvah, made of similar ingredients mixed with honey and served as dessert, proved far more successful.

On the second evening, a storm hit our vessel. Everything slid around, crashing onto the floor; chairs, tables, crockery – the lot. Simply walking along the narrow corridors became a balancing act. We all did the most sensible thing and retired to our tiny cabins, hoping that by morning the wind would subside and the waves cease their relentless banging on the sides of our poor, old, groaning ship.

I woke to quiet, peaceful rocking and, on peeping out of the porthole, saw clear blue skies. Trying to rouse my cabin-mates proved an impossible task. All I got were varying degrees of moans. I was starving, so, after quickly dressing, made my way to the dining hall to discover that I was the only passenger ready for breakfast. Virtually all the other travellers had been seasick during the night. I never managed to work out whether the stomach upsets resulted from the storm, or were due to our new Mediterranean diet or a bit of both. Maybe my early adventures had provided me with a stronger constitution.

Breakfast has always been my favourite meal. What an experience it was, sitting on my own in the large dining room; as much food as I could cope with, no hassle, no queues, just an abundance of food. The only others around were the sailors on duty, drinking 'coloured liquids' they called tea and coffee.

The last two or three days of the journey were uneventful in comparison. The dining room filled up more and more each day, and I lost the luxury of individual attention. Worse still, we had to queue for food, which was shoved on our plates ever more unceremoniously. It was during this trip that I received my first lesson on how not to stand in a queue – an art I never perfected but one the Israelis are experts at. It reminds me of the time, quite recently, when I gave a talk about the Kindertransport at a Jewish women's group's luncheon. During the buffet break, as I quietly waited at the back for the ladies to take their food, one of the organisers enquired why I wasn't eating.

'Ladies first,' I responded.

'Don't be so silly,' she retorted. 'If you wait any longer there won't be any food left.'

She needn't have worried; being a Jewish affair there was plenty.

On the final night, the crew suggested we get up early in order not to miss our first glimpse of the Holy Land. Standing on deck in semi-darkness, I began wondering what exactly would be visible through the torrential rain streaming down. Dawn broke and despite the lack of sun, sighting the shore of Israel against the background of the first shafts of light peeping over Mount Carmel was dramatic and heart-warming. I had never seen anything like it before.

White buildings strewn along its slopes, peeking out between multitudes of Lebanon cedar trees was indeed a sight to behold. Above them the Baha'i Temple, adorned with its impressive Gold Dome, stood majestically on the upper reaches of the mountain. Surrounding the temple on all sides were the most beautiful gardens in the middle of which lay steps leading straight up to the main entrance. At least the vast sums of money spent to celebrate this particular religion, emanating from Persia, was in aid of a benign deity, not one out to destroy all others.

It was the 8th February 1949 and we had just docked in Haifa.

It was colder and wetter than when we had left England some three weeks earlier which was my first surprise. Unusual weather we were quickly informed. Looking down from the deck, I noticed crowds of people dressed in a way I had never seen before. The Arab keffiyeh headdress for example was totally alien to me. I had only just managed to come to terms with the Jewish skull cap, the kippah, before leaving London.

Amongst the people in the throng alongside the boat, I easily picked out my Uncle Dolphie, Auntie's husband, whom I had met in London when he had visited. Dolphie Lovenson would have been difficult to miss, being tall, well-built, and immaculately dressed.

For me the most exciting part of being collected by Uncle Dolphie was his car - a Ford convertible. What more could a young teenage boy want? We drove up Mount Carmel, with views across the bay that even through the mist and rain looked stunning. In the distance the port of Akko, one of the oldest cities in the world, scene of Crusader battles and the location for the beginning of Napoleon's demise in the Middle East. Still further along, way into the distant horizon and somewhat hidden behind the clouds but towering above the Hills of Galilee, stood snow-capped Mount Hermon. Somewhere along its slopes is one of the sources of the river Jordan, whose holy waters have a lot to answer for. We continued past the Baha'i Temple to Uncle and Auntie's flat, located behind the shops of central Carmel.

Auntie, elegantly dressed as usual, and beautifully made up, was there to welcome me with a great hug. Looking at the structure of her face more closely she again conjured up the image of Ingrid Bergman – someone who on first sight fills you with admiration but from a slight distance leaves you never quite sure how close a relationship you will ever form with her.

Entering the room, I was met with the dining table laden with mounds of food and drink. Isn't that what all children yearn for? I nearly ate myself sick with chocolate, not the best in the world but still rationed in England when we left.

I was not yet fourteen, but for the second time in my life I had made another huge voyage to a strange land. But again, things didn't turn out as expected. Sadly, my stay at Auntie's didn't last long. Dolphie was an only child married to my Aunt Irene, a beautiful woman who adored and fussed over him. They had no children of their own although I am sure Irene would have made a wonderful, caring and loving mother

Auntie with my second child, Allon

A young teenager suddenly entering their home was bound to disturb the equilibrium. The flat had only one bedroom, which meant I slept in the sitting room. It quickly turned into a case of three being a crowd. Being a growing lad and invariably hungry I frequently raided the fridge, which unfortunately didn't go down well with Dolphie. Particularly when I unwittingly consumed the last piece of food he happened to be fond of.

I wonder too if the fact that Irene shared some of her affection with me created sparks of jealousy. He was an extremely clever man, spoke five or six languages fluently, had a great knowledge of the world at large – mostly, I would say, through rather 'blue-tinted' glasses – and was a fantastic Scrabble player. Dolphie had a phenomenal collection of mystery books, which I loved to read, although always careful to put them back in exactly the same place I'd originally found them. The only communication between us was our occasional games of Scrabble, and that probably only happened because he always beat me. His firm, Traders and Shippers, which he created and ran with his life-long friend and partner, Theodore, was a financial success; consequently, money never seemed much of an issue.

During my first few months in Israel I met up several times with my oldest brother, Jacques. Since he had found me in Dorking we had seen each other occasionally – at Uncle Izzi's in London, at the Habonim farm in Bosham near Chichester, and at his wedding in Manchester to his first wife, Jean. Jacques and Jean had volunteered to fight in the 1948 Israeli War of Independence and had considered settling there. But by the time I arrived, they had decided to return to England. They needed to sell their belongings in order to raise cash. They had brought with them, amongst other items, hundreds of classical records. Somehow my dear brother persuaded me to catalogue the lot which took me hours of tedious labour. To be fair though, this rather boring task allowed me to discover a whole new world of music, and the names of composers, many of whom I had never heard of before.

During one of Jacques' expeditions to sell their possessions we met our father's closest brother in age, Josef, who lived in Nesher, just outside Haifa. An entirely new world opened up. Most of his family came directly from Poland. My father, Schapse, the youngest of nine, was, I believe, one of the only siblings to venture out of Poland as a young man, long before the war. This included, at one point, travelling to Palestine where he served for a period in the Palestine Police. On his way back, via Vienna, he met Mina, my mother. Of my father's brothers and sisters only three or four, out of the nine of them, had survived.

It was to my uncle Josef that my parents sent their last communication, a Red Cross telegram from the Warsaw ghetto, dated May 1942. 'We are fine; the boys are in England, let our in-laws, Lovenzon in Haifa know.'

I still have the original telegram in my possession. Every time I look at it my mind takes a leap, wondering what it must have been like, cooped-up, poverty-stricken, with little or no food, inside the Ghetto, scared and under constant threat of death. All the while, speculating, worrying what was happening to their three young offspring and wondering if they would ever see them again.

I'm pretty sure Jacques succeeded in selling most of his possessions. I know that Josef took some of the kitchen equipment, but then my brother was, and remains, a salesman 'par excellence'. Always in total command of his product knowledge and able to answer any question, however trivial.

Meanwhile, back in Haifa, the serious matter of finding a school for me was in full swing. Dolphie had already made enquiries for me to go to Mishmar Haemek – a kibbutz near Haifa where there was a boarding school.

First, of course, was the small matter of learning Hebrew. Have you ever tried absorbing a new language where not only the letters are strange but you also have to read the sentences in the reverse direction? To make life even more complicated, the letters are different in print than when written in script and, topping it all, most books and newspapers dispense with the vowels. Irene, in the sixty-odd years she lived in Haifa, never managed to overcome these linguistic obstacles. There was really no need. For many years one of the main languages spoken in Haifa's central Carmel cafes remained German.

For me the situation was somewhat different. After all, how could I attend school without understanding the country's language? I'd had to overcome that hurdle once before, so this shouldn't be too much of an ordeal, or so I thought. I couldn't really remember my first upheaval of being thrown headlong into a new culture and strange language in England. For this teenager it was to prove quite different, and certainly more memorable than for the four-year-old ten years earlier.

As so often happens in life, matters were resolved by chance. Jacques and Jean had already returned to London when I received an invitation to my father's sister, Malka's son's wedding – he being my cousin, Efraim. On entering their house, where the reception was being held, everybody looked at me, exclaiming: 'Ah! Schapse's youngest.' Momentarily, I was taken aback, not quite knowing how to respond. I just kept nodding my head in affirmation. Very few spoke or understood English; my Hebrew was still practically non-existent but we managed to communicate in a sort of German/Yiddish. In amongst the wedding guests, however, there was one person who spoke English reasonably well. He, it transpired, was a second cousin who lived in Kibbutz Merchavya, located in the Jezrael Valley near Afula, which had a school attached, taking in boarders. Hey presto! A solution. *I'll learn Hebrew faster, Dolphie will no doubt breathe a sigh of relief, and I'll be on the move again.*

As far as I was concerned a new school and a cousin, albeit one I had only met once before, was sufficient. And that was what happened. I was to go to school and live on Kibbutz Merchavya.

Even though I knew nothing of what a kibbutz was!

Chapter Six

Kibbutz, aged 14-18

The only way by which any one divests himself
of his natural liberty and puts on
the bonds of civil society is by
agreeing with other men
to join and unite into a community

John Locke (1632-1704)

The kibbutz - where do I start? Well, I first set foot in
Kibbutz Merchavya in the summer holidays, during a heat
wave. Mind you, every summer turned out to be a heat
wave as far as I was concerned. It was, so I had been
informed, an idyllic community where everyone was equal
and all the members shared everything with their fellow
kibbutz members. Not quite, but it could have been. For a
start, some members came with belongings others could
only hope for. Then there were those who received German
restitution money and yet another group whose parents,
living in town, sent them a few 'extras'. On the whole
though, during those early pioneering days, the system
proved pretty egalitarian. Both men and women worked
for the community, while children were looked after in
their own quarters and slept separately from their parents,
virtually from birth.

The ideological theory was that men and women were
equal and therefore could both be employed doing the

same work, whether physical or otherwise. While many women did labour in the fields, in reality the majority were involved in looking after children, working in the central laundry, cooking and taking responsibility for the communal dining hall – not so original really. Nevertheless, the very idea of physical labour being accessible to those who fought for it created a new atmosphere; one in which at least an effort was made to uphold the equality of the sexes. This, we should also remember, was in an era in which the image of the suffragette of the 1920s still cast a mystical shadow over society.

It was on the kibbutz that I discovered to my delight that being a good Jew doesn't necessarily imply having to have ultra-religious beliefs. In fact, I learned that most of the festivals revolve around the agricultural seasons. It was a revelation to find that Passover could be regarded as a festival of freedom, with or without the ten plagues and that these probably had a natural explanation if one bothered to delve a little deeper into the ways of nature. Nobody in the kibbutz fasted on Yom Kippur, it being a purely religious occasion. Anyway, I suspect that most of the kibbutzniks felt they had no need of absolution for sins they may or may not have committed.

I never forgot those early kibbutz lessons and have come to regard many of our ancient customs still practised today, whether under purely religious auspices or otherwise, as part of my Jewish heritage and history. So, despite being a rare visitor to the synagogue, I love the magical Jewish past, filled with battles against the odds, murders and deceptions, all wrapped in a mystical aura.

It was many years later, just after I returned to live in England, that I was asked to meet my oldest son Allon's Hebrew teacher at the Jewish primary school he was then attending. 'Erich,' the Israeli teacher said, beginning the conversation in Hebrew. 'I simply can't understand you. You speak fluent Hebrew, your son gets all the questions right in any Jewish history test, yet you are not religious.'

'It just goes to prove,' I responded, 'that it isn't a prerequisite to view everything only through a religious lens in order to understand and appreciate one's background.'

I fell short of telling him that when we went to football on Saturdays, Allon usually asked me not to drive past the synagogue. That was his concession to the faith.

The kibbutz was, and to a degree probably still is, a fascinating sociological phenomenon; created partially out of ideology, and not a little out of necessity. The initial concept belonged to the refugees from Eastern Europe and Russia, fleeing the violent and ever-increasing pogroms. They had an overriding ambition to create a new life based on working the soil. Where better than in the biblical 'Promised Land', from which we had been ousted some two thousand years ago? There was land available, mainly swamps and desert. However, there were also indigenous inhabitants scattered around trying to cultivate some of the barren countryside, albeit with old-fashioned and primitive implements. The Palestinians weren't enamoured of the gradual influx of a population who regarded their ancient roots stemming from the same country. The inevitable frictions resulted in the immigrants defending themselves at the same time as trying to create their new vision. Not an easy concept, particularly if one bears in mind the fact that physical, agricultural labour was alien to most previous Jewish generations, since as far back as the destruction of the second Temple and the final Exodus.

The idea of a community working as one unit provided part of the solution. The kibbutz population, never more than four percent of the total inhabitants living in Israel, made a contribution – disproportionate to its numbers – to the safety, security, welfare and essential food production of the country. This was particularly relevant in the early days of the State and during the various wars with its Arab neighbours. It undoubtedly proved an extraordinary social phenomenon, possibly not really given the credit it deserved. The truth is, of all the communal settlements established around the world over centuries under a variety of different guises, the kibbutz system developed into as near a real communal society as human nature would allow. A system in which members enjoyed similar standards of living but where it was not obligatory to become absolute slaves to rigid rules or quasi-mystical, religious laws. It is one of the longest-lasting, ideological, communal societies in history. I still have inner feelings of sadness and regret that so few of us were capable of surviving its potentially unique way of life, an existence I personally found satisfying, despite its shortcomings. It constituted a sort of extended family which, unfortunately at times, became somewhat intrusive and therefore hard to come to terms with.

Much happened to me during my eight-year sojourn in Merchavya. I changed from a fourteen-year-old boy to a young man of twenty-two. It was a journey of discovery, from puberty to young adulthood, not quite to maturity. I well remember my conspicuous arrival, on a steaming hot summer day. Auntie Irene had driven me to the kibbutz in the Ford convertible. On arrival, we were quickly surrounded by youngsters on all sides. Convertibles were rare in Israel and on a kibbutz unimaginable. Luckily, my cousin Eliezer, hearing the commotion, came down to greet us. As I viewed the crowd around the car, my heart sank. How was I going to explain my genteel Viennese Aunt and her luxury car? Eliezer and his charming wife, Urge, quickly took control, shepherding us up to their small room. There they made us feel welcome with a sort of coffee, in Hebrew called Botz (mud), which was exactly what it initially tasted like, and biscuits.

As it happens, even when I go to Israel these days, I still ask for Botz. It's a kind of blend between Turkish and Arab coffee. It reminds me of those early days. Having overcome this initial hurdle, my worries turned to the more serious and pressing problem of how I was going to survive this totally new and alien way of life? Never mind the heat, and the mosquitoes that seemed to have acquired an immediate crush on me – more to the point, how was I ever going to overcome yet another apparently insurmountable language barrier?

After Irene returned to Haifa I was proudly shown around the kibbutz, which possessed a number of large old buildings constructed by the first wave of immigrants, around the turn of the twentieth century. Most were now used for the kibbutz's laundry and offices. The members' living quarters were located in a more leafy area. Then, of course, the obligatory tour of the cowsheds, chicken runs, goat pens, and tractor parks; and the accompanying, unfamiliar – and pretty odious – smells which, in time, I became used to. Finally, we made our way to the school living quarters which consisted of separate one-storey buildings incorporating six bedrooms, each with three or four beds. Toilets and showers were at the end of the open corridor. After taking me to my designated room and pointing out my bed, Eliezer suggested I unpack, have a shower and return to his room from where we'd go together to the dining hall, for supper.

Having sorted out my luggage, towel in hand, I proceeded to the showers. Imagine my surprise and horror while happily standing under a cold shower when four girls walked in, calmly undressed, and stood in the cubicles beside me. So immersed in their conversation, none of them appeared to notice this shy, pale, scrawny youngster desperately crouching, trying to hide his wares. I cringed, grabbed my towel and ran for dear life; their mocking laughter ringing in my ears as I scrambled into the corridor to the comparative safety of my room. Little did I know I was sharing the room with two girls and another boy. It was all just a bit too much for a young teenager from English suburbia. Despite the trauma, I calmed down and, thankfully, didn't descend into some kind of sexual denial. Once I mastered the language a little, we all became good friends and learned to turn around when a roommate of the opposite sex was getting dressed.

Quite uncanny how quickly we are able to adapt to new ways of life. Couples from the same class were rarely formed; we knew each other far too well and were more like siblings, with all the heated arguments that are part and parcel of that kind of relationship, rather than potential partners.

My real problem during those first months was learning and understanding Hebrew. Every time I tried to utter a new phrase, invariably incorrectly, either in the wrong gender or in a peculiar accent, the word went on my joke list. Fortunately, it grew so quickly that after a time the first phrases were dropped in order to include the new, juicier, utterances. These were recited back to me - usually when I was about to fall asleep. The idea, I presume, was to give me the odd nightmare or two.

It's a wonder I ever became fluent in Hebrew. But despite these odds, I did and I still am.

Not long after arriving, we went on a weekend jaunt to the Kinneret (Sea of Galilee). The heat was unbearable. I spent most of my time in the water trying to cool down and eating watermelons, neither of which I was used to. Consequently, on returning, I was violently sick. My vomiting was compounded by a high temperature. I tried to explain to the nurse, and those prepared to listen, that I felt dizzy and generally disoriented. Not knowing any of the appropriate words, I searched around for a way to describe how I felt. 'You see up there,' I mumbled, pointing to the full moon. 'It's just like that, everything seems so far away.' The roars of laughter that followed were excruciating and made yet a further dent in my already low linguistic self-esteem.

School was yet another eye-opener — no such thing as tests or exams. Everything hinged on self-discipline. If you wanted to learn, and do the little homework that was set, all well and good. If not, a gentle chastising was the worst you could expect. The same applied during the actual lessons. The teacher would quietly ask you to 'shut up' so that those who wanted to learn, and discover something about the world, could do so. It was a far cry from the discipline of Dorking Grammar School - more like heaven on earth.

It was not unusual, for example, that during English lessons, from which I was exempt, I would be found playing basketball with several classmates, who had not been excused and whose knowledge of the English language was non-existent. I happen to believe it was too young an age for children to be self-motivated, on the other hand the kibbutz education system, with a little tweaking, is probably preferable to the non-stop exams children are confronted with today. For us youngsters at the time, it was a wonderful and free world.

A number of teachers stood out and made an indelible mark on my life. First there was Bozik, our music teacher. His love for Berlioz and his *Symphonie Fantastique*, which he dissected bar-by-bar over many months, is something I have never forgotten. The wonders of the story of unrequited love, and the glorious music accompanying it, were like an emotional magnet to my senses. The ominous *March to the Scaffold* still sends goose pimples down my spine. I believe Bozik's son later became a music conductor, including, at one point at the Amsterdam Concertgebouw.

Then there was Buma, a tall, broad and extraordinarily clever man who taught us that the Old Testament, despite some inaccuracies, vivid religious imagination and over-simplification, should be regarded as a pretty good reflection of Jewish history. He reminded us that it wasn't a holy transcript to be learned off by heart, and swallowed lock, stock and barrel, but should be studied as an early record of the Jewish people – a view I have retained, and believe still holds fast.

It was Tuvia, our erudite school librarian, whose morbid fascination for Goethe opened up the world of literature. The whole idea of Faust selling his soul to the devil for the love of a beautiful and unattainable woman intrigued him and, boy, did he let us know. Tuvia and I frequently met in the library where, to begin with, we communicated in German. Little by little though, Hebrew became our main language of conversation. Apart from his intimate knowledge of German literature, he was also a lover of poetry, introducing us to the modern Israeli poet Bialik, as well as Pushkin, Byron and Shakespeare, the latter, difficult enough in the original language, was virtually incomprehensible when translated into Hebrew.

I vividly recall the occasion he took us to a Hebrew version of Steinbeck's *Of Mice and Men*, at the Habima Theatre in Tel Aviv. It was there I first heard 'Good Night Irene', which much later became the lullaby for my children before lights out. In retrospect, Tuvia's influence helped me discover and appreciate the beauty and depth of the written word.

I shall forever be indebted to these teachers who guided me into trying to understand what lies behind the written word, how to appreciate music and be able to delve into one's historic background with an open mind. Imagine all this without one test or exam.

When I arrived in Merchavya as a pupil my name was Erich, the one given me at birth by my parents. This was not 'English' enough for the 'Sabras' – the Israeli-born children – so they hunted around for weeks, trying to work out a more appropriate tag. Then suddenly, while watching the weekly film, the solution was found. The film we were watching was *Tarzan the Ape Man*, with Johnny Weissmuller. Johnny Weissmuller, I became. The surname was quickly dropped once it was discovered I couldn't swim, never mind swing on trees or even play a decent game of football.

Johnny remained the name I was known by for years, and many of my old close friends still call me that. Although I respond to both, depending on which I am addressed by, my emotional response to the one or the other is never quite the same. I suppose the nickname acquired as a teenager instinctively turns the clock back to that period. Erich, the name I was given at birth, signifies at one and the same time my original close family, of which I remember little, and a later era altogether. At the time, of course, it produced, like the chameleon, another layer, another means of changing my self-image.

I experienced several lifestyle changes on Kibbutz Merchavya. For example, lessons were from early morning till lunch, six days a week. After lunch, and a short siesta, we were set two to three hours' physical labour, presumably to prepare us for a future working on the land. During this, we could find ourselves anywhere from cleaning out muck in the cowsheds and collecting eggs from the chicken runs – where I had a near-collision with a poisonous snake – to picking fruit in the fields or, worst of all, an evening shift in the communal dining room, washing a never-ending number of dishes. One of the jobs, by far the most boring, was taking the sheep out to graze. It was so dull, I frequently found myself sitting on a hard rock and allowing my imagination to run amok. It's quite wonderful how, in the world of make believe, the vision becomes so clear. No obstacles are there to be confronted; no grey clouds appear to obscure the way to exciting individual achievements and the ultimate path to one's personal heaven.

Apart from imagining being the world's fastest long-distance runner and, in the process, winning an Olympic medal, as part of day-dreaming I used to, and occasionally still do, hum a variety of melodies. One of these tunes made such an impression on me that for several months I truly believed that it was my creation and of extraordinarily high musical quality. I was partly right, all the sadder that Mozart had composed it a hundred and fifty years earlier as the third movement of his fifth violin concerto, *The Turkish*.

I can't imagine what the poor sheep must have made of the boy standing among them waving his hand in the air. They certainly didn't respond in orchestral unison. It was more a case of dancing away in sheer bewilderment. You could say this was not my favourite part of kibbutz education. It wasn't that I minded physical work, it was more an issue of utter boredom; trying to look after and move animals who simply stared at you, refused to budge, just continuing to incessantly chew the little dry grass, or hay, left on the ground. Reading books, listening to the radio or playing basketball were considerably more attractive occupations for me as a teenager.

Meat was scarce, and aubergine was the accepted substitute. It came in every form imaginable; as goulash, schnitzel, steak and even in the shape of some peculiar type of sausage. Mind you, despite becoming pretty monotonous, aubergines do, I understand, provide a very nourishing element of any diet. Could this be an aspect of life where the kibbutz was ahead of its time – again, more by force of circumstance than as a result of ideology, of course?

What, I wonder, would those preachers of strict vegan, vegetarian, organic and whole-food make of it all? Maybe, a balanced diet of food and ideology, flexible and capable of bending with the ever-changing conditions we are so frequently confronted with, is a more appropriate way to lead a healthy and honest life?

Around the age of sixteen I was confronted with yet another change. Up until then I used to go 'home' to Aunt Irene in Haifa for the holidays, and remember well the year when Israel was covered in snow, all the way south down to the Negev Desert. I happened to be in Haifa at the time. With snowdrifts of up to half-a-metre deep, I was suddenly, happily snow-bound for nearly a week. Unfortunately, it was also then that dear Uncle Dolphie began to realise that my left-wing views were far too extreme for his taste. What exactly he expected, sending me to board at an ideologically left-wing kibbutz I can't imagine. Merchavya was the home of Meir Yaari, the leader of Mapam, the most radical party in Israel bar the Communists.

On several occasions, I interpreted for Meir Yaari when dignitaries from abroad turned up unexpectedly. The occasion of a meeting with an Indian minister proved pretty hairy. For a start, I had great difficulty understanding his broad Indian accent, which wasn't made any easier by the speed at which the words came hurtling toward me. To make matters worse, Meir Yaari was, like most Eastern European Israelis, impatient. He couldn't tolerate more than a split-second between the word being uttered and its Hebrew interpretation. I didn't live up to his expectations and was never invited to interpret again – nor did I, as a result of this experience, consider taking up linguistics or interpreting as a profession.

On these visits 'home', if politics was discussed I believe Dolphie found my views much too radical. He considered that I should leave boarding at the school on Kibbutz Merchavya to be away from communist influence and go to an agricultural college in Pardess Katz, somewhere in the middle of the country. Patently I made a good impression when I visited, as I was offered a place immediately. The trouble was, yet again nobody had bothered to ask my views on the matter.

The truth is, I would have gladly returned to live with Irene and Dolphie in Haifa, and to be part of their family and social network. But to have to deal yet again with new and unfamiliar surroundings was a prospect I just could not bear. I was very upset but too shy to express my concerns directly to Dolphie or Irene. I returned to Merchavya and explained the situation to Eliezer and Urge. They had already taken me under their wing as my 'kibbutz parents'. After much discussion, it was decided to ask the kibbutz to keep me on as a potential future member, even if no further payments were forthcoming. I rang Auntie and informed her of my decision to stay at the kibbutz. The consequences came as quite a shock. All communication with my aunt and uncle ceased until my military service two years later. Dolphie hardly ever spoke to me again and, from that time up until his death, kept his distance, rarely acknowledged my existence.

The following two years included a few more scrapes, including the odd hospitalisation for minor injuries, such as cutting open my kneecap, and suffering an electric shock from overhead electric wires while moving aluminium water pipes. One incident that does stick out, however, is the time I was asked to accompany the night-time, milk-run driver to Tel Aviv.

All went well until, on the return journey, at about three in the morning and around twenty kilometres from home and in the pitch dark, the engine conked out. The pump had given up. The driver's solution was for me to sit on the front wheel's mud-guard and hand pump. Well, by the time we arrived home an hour or so later I could hardly move my aching arm, and the rest of my body was pretty stiff, too, virtually frozen. Every time I travel along that part of the road, in the middle of the relatively desolate Wadi Ara, my muscles begin to twitch.

During this period, communication with Emilie, my foster mother in Dorking, continued by letter on a sort of regular basis. I missed having her care, warmth and affection near at hand. It had been such a vital part of my childhood and upbringing. At the same time, although only sporadically, I kept in touch with my brothers, both married with children and with their own problems to contend with. Jacques was living in Australia, while Ossie was in London. As siblings, none of us really had any idea what the other was experiencing. It was as if we weren't really part of the same family, just three boys who happened to have been born to the same set of parents and had been torn apart by circumstances totally beyond our control and were consequently, although thankfully alive, now devoid of a central focus to hold us together as a unit.

Time and again my mind returns to wondering about what kind of life I would now be leading but for the Holocaust. Yet, despite instinctively yearning to make up for those lost years and create a close-knit family of my own, I have unfortunately, in family terms, managed to achieve the opposite. Somehow, the need has been so great that I seem to keep on over-compensating, and lose the very thing I strive for so ardently.

Meanwhile, as I approached eighteen, all roads were fast leading not to higher education, or building a family of my own.

The Israeli army was beckoning me.

Chapter Seven

Israeli Army, aged 18-21

> These are the times that try men's souls. The summer
> soldier and the sunshine patriot will, in this crisis,
> shrink from the service of their country; but he that
> stands it now, deserves the love and thanks of men
> and women.

Thomas Paine, The Crisis

My army service, two-and-a-half years long with a little
tacked on for the 1956 Suez Campaign, felt like a lifetime.
To this day when I get together with friends who also did
army service in Israel we still talk about the things that
happened to us during that period. The near misses, the
jokes and, of course, the obligatory hardships we were all
made to suffer. Army service very quickly turns into an
artificial way of life. On the one hand, transitory, not quite
real, on the other, confrontation with the enemy, frequently
a matter of life and death.

I've come to the conclusion that the army is one of
society's ancient institutions set up to prove the theory of
'survival of the fittest' in every sense. Which of course begs
the question, how do we define the fittest? Is it those who
can defend themselves best or the ones that are the most
aggressive toward their neighbours? Certainly, in those
early days of the state of Israel, survival was uppermost in
our minds. I imagine for most eighteen-year-olds the

sudden change from a warm caring home and a regular educational routine to a military regime must be quite traumatic. The kibbutz environment from which I had come, however, seemed to smooth the path a little. We were used to being independent, frequently obliged to navigate our own way on the many treks we took along the hills of Galilee or in the searing heat of the Negev Desert. Hard work and endurance were also no strangers to us. It's not surprising, therefore, to find that a high percentage of kibbutz kids became pilots, volunteered for the paratroopers, worked in intelligence or completed their army service as officers. It does appear to indicate that a more relaxed attitude to academia, combined with a physical work ethic, can produce unusually positive results.

Being good democratic kibbutzniks we had a meeting before 'D' Day and agreed to stick together even if some of us would have preferred to try for the air force or volunteer for other areas in the forces. Collective responsibility and majority rule was our motto. It served us right that, as a result, we found ourselves in one of the most dreaded ground regiments: Givati.

A rude awakening it turned out to be. What would you feel like if, on your very first day of service, a sergeant half your size poked a stick in your midriff and barked, 'Reich! So that there are no misunderstandings, you are here for the duration. Your only way out earlier is either on a stretcher or in an ambulance. Got it?'

'Yes, Sir!'

What else could I say?

In the Israeli Army (1954)

It was a dramatic start to our three-month initiation course and it took us several weeks to acclimatise to our new surroundings and change of lifestyle, by which time even the sparse conditions of the kibbutz conjured the illusion of glorious luxury. We'd enrolled toward the end of September so were spared some of the intense heat of summer. Instead we found ourselves crawling through heavy mud in full gear knowing that if our dear sergeant found so much as a speck on our rifles the whole exercise would start all over again.

Not being the most agile, I soon acquired intimate knowledge of the crawling course and, in the process, lost much of my youthful appearance and weight. The first positive break came some two months into our strict and somewhat debilitating regime. My home, Kibbutz Merchavya, is located between the valleys of Jeezrel and Beth Shaan, scenes of many biblical stories. These include the hanging of Jonathan, close friend of David, and Jonathan's father King Saul, at the gates of Beth Shaan. One of the region's major geographical landmarks, Mount Tabor, is a stand-alone hill boasting a rounded top, visible from virtually all parts of the region. It's also a significant and well-known ancient site mentioned in both the Old and New Testaments. According to the former, it was here that the armies gathered under the guidance of the prophetess Deborah to fight Sisera. In the latter it marks the traditional place where the scene of the Transfiguration is said to have taken place.

At the time of our army service there was an annual ten-kilometre race around the slopes of Mount Tabor, in memory of Yitzhak Sadeh, one of Israel's early military heroes. Shaul, a classmate of mine, and I dreamed up the idea of applying for a weekend pass to participate in the run, which would allow us to go home and also to be the first to obtain a pass out of camp. Somewhat to our surprise we were granted our wish. On the journey home, our main discussions revolved around 'to run or not to run' but as both of us actually enjoyed this sporting activity we decided to participate. Lucky we did. After returning to camp we were called to the commanding officer who, unbeknown to us, had served with Sadeh in the War of Independence. He informed us that while coming sixth and ninth was quite respectable, if we wished to run again the next time he would expect improved performances. I doubt I had the ability to run any better and, anyway, this was one challenge I was not planning to repeat, so it really didn't matter. We had achieved our aims of getting a break from the hard grind, and being home for a night.

The preliminary course over, we were dispersed across different parts of the army. I found myself enrolled on a corporal's course based near the small biblical town of Beth Gubrin. Located between the Mediterranean port of Ashkelon and Jerusalem it presumably acted as the first line of the defences for the ancient capital against the Philistine infidels scattered along the coast. Ashkelon was one of their major cities, known for its connection with Samson and so evocatively portrayed in David's lament at the death of his beloved Jonathan.

O Jonathan, in your death I am stricken,
I am desolate for you, Jonathan my brother,
Very dear to me you were,

Your love to me more wonderful
than the love of a woman
How the mighty have fallen (Jonathan's
Father Saul)
Tell it not in Gat,
Proclaim it not in the streets of Ashkelon;
Lest the daughters of the Philistines rejoice.

Living in Israel one is constantly confronted with stories from the Bible and its long history – so full of life, beauty, corruption, cruelty, and, above all, a sense of humanity. David's *Psalms* and the later *Song of Solomon* are surely reminiscent of sonnets, poems and literature found three thousand years later in the works of the literary giants we so admire today. At that time, religion and a supernatural deity were, no doubt, crucial in calming the daily fears of war, natural disasters, starvation and death from sudden illnesses, for which no explanations or remedies existed. My difficulty is trying to come to terms with the obsessive desire, thousands of years later, to seek narrow religious interpretations of these early writings, then somehow transpose the same rules from a long-gone, ancient era to modern-day life, as if the intervening centuries didn't exist or teach us anything.

David, thousands of years ago, didn't confine his outpourings only to religious premises. In the *Song of the Bow*, for example, God is not mentioned at all. The sonnet describes real people, comparing the skills of Jonathan and Saul to the strengths of animals, not to an unknown deity whose powers can't be tested or challenged. The lament for Jonathan expresses a profound love for another human being, which may or may not have had sexual overtones. His affection for Jonathan was expressed in earthly human terms, which even transcended the knowledge that Jonathan's father Saul hated David and wished for his death. I'm getting a bit carried away, I suppose, but it gets rather complicated trying to untangle the vibrant strands of the past that run through the present on into the future. Especially when one is in a country surrounded by so many ancient monuments, most of which are mentioned in the Bible.

My new camp turned out to be within walking distance of Tel Lachish, an ancient settlement, reduced to ruins and rubble centuries ago. Long before the times of David and Goliath, a thriving town breathed and existed there. Joshua erased it soon after entering the Promised Land from Mount Nebo. Much, much later it became the last staging-post for Nebuchadnezzar, Emperor of Persia, on his way to capturing Jerusalem, thus setting in motion one of the first Jewish wanderings from the Promised Land. It also provided Verdi with a wonderful setting for his opera *Nabucco*, for which he composed the famous 'Chorus of the Hebrew Slaves' which was used to promote Italian nationalism in the nineteenth century. Living in the midst of these numerous historic sites, earth mounds and archaeological ruins, one becomes aware that every stone is an integral part of one's heritage – all roads lead not to Rome but back to the Bible.

The course at Beth Gubrin proved to be another mental and physical ordeal. I managed to lose a few more kilos during our weeks of training, and by the time we had completed the three months' special programme I felt a close and intimate affiliation with every nook and cranny of every wadi and hill along the lower slopes of Jerusalem. I never realised how many actually existed. Nor did I have the time or inclination to appreciate the sheer beauty of my surroundings. We'd crawl up yet another mound, certain it was the last, only to find there were many more even higher, some stretching way into the distant horizon.

Not being the best of navigators, I was known to lose my bearings occasionally. This meant finding my own way back to camp, where I would arrive in the early hours of the morning when most of my colleagues were fast asleep. I improved considerably as time went on and mainly because I gained self-belief and a confidence in my ability to make quick, instinctive, first-time decisions, to the point where reading maps, looking for new routes and short cuts along uneven local terrain became a bit of a hobby. Many years later I was forever gazing at maps in search of inspirational new itineraries and routes on which to send my unsuspecting charity fund-raisers.

Nine months into military service I became a corporal, and the proud owner of two stripes. It didn't take long to find out how meaningless this initial step up the army ladder really was. My first assignment turned out to be an experience I could have happily lived without. It might have been considered humorous at the time if the events had it not been so frightening and the consequences so tragic. I was attached to a brigade training in one of the most isolated spots one can possibly find in Israel. The unit was called 'The Old Timers Brigade'. On arriving, and peering through the swirling sand and dust clouds, I had my first glimpse of what lay ahead. The explanation for the unit's name was quite simple and innovative. The soldiers in this light-hearted, 'glamorous' brigade had, at one time or another during their military service, spent time in prison. The rule is clear – time used skiving off from the army in this fashion is not regarded as part of normal, obligatory national military service. Learning this information sent my heartbeat racing.

A few days after arriving, I discovered that my worst fears were indeed well-founded. I was the 'freshman', the one with the least experience of army life. Although I had already completed my first nine months, some of these poor guys hadn't even got through their first three months' training, despite being in the army for over a year. It didn't take long to realise I was in for a rough ride. Just thinking back, I realise hauling them out of bed in the morning had been much more difficult than later getting some of my children up on a school day. Cold water generously poured over them tended to produce better results than cursing or shouting.

The first real crisis came when I was informed by the commanding officer that it was high time my subordinates had haircuts. He was, of course, right. They looked a real scraggy lot, but it begged the question: why had this simple task been left for such a long time?

I discovered the reason in no time. The barber was sitting patiently waiting for his first customer, a most reluctant old-timer who, with some considerable cajoling, I eventually managed to persuade that he couldn't really afford to refuse my offer. The second in line point-blank refused to co-operate, explaining volubly, and in pretty rude, crude, language what he thought of me. For a few seconds I was stumped, but being rather naïve as to how to tackle such situations, I informed the errant soldier that he was about to be reported to the senior officer. I barely had time to turn around when somebody shouted: 'Drop, quick!'

I was in the process of falling and hitting the ground when a body, bayonet in hand, came flying over me. Somewhat shaken, I watched as he was escorted away for yet another term in prison, and a few extra months were added to his army service.

Shock apart, I felt pretty helpless and somewhat dejected. What should I have done? It was as if, for these veterans at least, having their hair shorn and taking orders from their juniors was synonymous with giving up part of their manhood; echoes of Samson perhaps, except I was no Delilah. Had she been available the whole platoon would no doubt have acquiesced with alacrity.

I went to visit my assailant in prison and asked him what it was all about. I didn't really get a coherent response but was made to understand that being ordered around by a young Ashkenazi whippersnapper wasn't acceptable to a veteran Sephardi like him. And anyway, he concluded, why didn't I try a bit harder to persuade rather than threatening to report him? For those not familiar with the terms, an Ashkenazi Jew is one whose ancestors are from Eastern Europe while Sephardi Jews came from Spain, Portugal, North Africa and the Middle East.

If that wasn't enough, two or three days later, just before sunrise and after the usual difficult, noisy, dawn wake-up call for another day's training – and the commencement of regular, mutual hostilities – a shot was heard from one of the small tents. My heart sank as I ran to investigate. Crawling through the open flap, I was confronted with the most awful scene: a young Romanian had shot himself. He was about twenty-one, short and slightly built, the only European amid a company of mostly North African émigrés – hardened men, used to fighting for their survival in a hostile environment and whose attitude to life was so different to that of this gentle, confused youngster. He had no chance and should never have been despatched to this brigade. What a waste and so very sad.

It took me years to shut out the picture of his head cradled in my arms as his life slowly ebbed away into nothingness. I thank my lucky stars that, despite becoming quite friendly with most of the squad, we were never put to the test in live military operation. I can't imagine how far, if at all, any of them would have followed me.

I must have done something right during the course at Beth Gubrin because my next assignment was to be sent back as an instructor – promoted to Sergeant. I left the veterans in the desert with no regrets. Much of the next period had different kinds of trials and tribulations. It coincided with the ever-increasing attacks by the Fedayeen (Arab militants) emanating mainly from the Egyptian-held Gaza Strip.

So, what's new? You may well ask.

Not quite suicide bombers, but the same devastating effect on the children in their school buses, or vehicles filled with unsuspecting passengers driving straight over booby-traps laid during the previous night. Our task involved, among other duties, night patrols along the borders including a few incursions into the Strip itself. The incident that remains etched in my mind was the time we were sent to check a fedayeen firing position, not far from the town of Khan Yunis. It was a cloudless night with a beautiful full moon, which at any other time would have proved irresistibly romantic. That night the mood was somewhat different. The moonlight shone over the near-white sand dunes giving the most extraordinary visibility for miles around. So not an easy task ahead, one that would, no doubt, require a lot of slow belly-crawling.

There were five of us in the patrol: a captain, a lieutenant, two course participants and myself. On reaching the border, imagine our surprise on seeing the captain fall to his knees, become immersed in deep prayer, and start motioning for us to continue. Three hours later we returned, having discovered the fedayeen's firing position by attracting a shower of bullets that screamed over our heads. Our dear captain was still kneeling, presumably now communicating directly with God. Nothing was ever mentioned about what had occurred that night. It was, however, a timely reminder that we are, after all, humans, each with his or her individual fears and trepidations.

At about this time, two of my friends – both members of different kibbutzim – and I were informed that we had been accepted onto the army officers' course, the caveat being that we'd have to remain in Beth Gubrin as instructors for a second course. It also meant it would be necessary to sign for at least a further nine months' military service. In order to enrol on the officers' course, it was obligatory to serve for at least one full year after completion. The three of us decided to discuss the matter with the commander of our unit, Colonel Bar Lev, later to become Commander-in-Chief of the Israeli army, and Minister for Law and Order in the Israeli Government. A lengthy debate ensued, the outcome of which was an unprecedented arrangement whereby it was agreed that we would stay as instructors then join the officers' course without having to sign on for further duty. I doubt a similar arrangement would be acceptable today.

I would say that instructing and leading younger recruits helps in gaining self-confidence. I always participated in the manoeuvres under the same conditions as the course participants. To the point that on one of the punishments I handed out for repeated lateness to duty, the entire platoon and I ran some ten kilometres over the hills with full backpack. We arrived back in pitch darkness, most of them huffing and puffing behind me. Apart from giving me great satisfaction for being in better physical nick than the rest of the platoon, I didn't have much trouble with their time-keeping after that.

I arrived at the officers' course base camp, located in the centre of the country not far from Ben Gurion airport, to be met by many familiar faces. Once our loud greetings and back-slapping were over, harsh reality was quickly restored. Having instructed on two courses, where I gave the orders and was shown some respect because I was the boss, it was pretty difficult to swap roles. Little time was given to adjust and as I graduated from one course or another my areas of weakness always managed to manifest themselves. This is presumably one of the main objectives of these physically and mentally challenging programmes. Embarrassment was also a feature.

The daily routine was fairly simple: wake up call, dress, wash, breakfast, tidy rooms, then full gear with spick and span uniforms ready for morning parade. All this activity started just before dawn, when most normal mortals are fast asleep. On the particular morning in question, after breakfast I suddenly had an urgent need for the toilet – the story of my life. On returning to my room, after visiting the toilet, I realised that if I tidied my bed, I'd be late for the precious morning parade, attracting all the consequences that this entailed. I hauled on my gear and ran for dear life. All went well, I wasn't even admonished for my shabby dress and unpolished shoes. Then came the sting. 'I will now show you how not to leave your room in the morning,' barked our commander to the entire company, standing to attention. We were marched into the room I slept in, past my bed and back out onto the parade ground. In line with the rest, I marched through my room, looked at the unmade bed and continued with the others back to the parade ground. I was mortified, with nowhere to hide and was the laughing stock – or so I thought. The truth is that most of the company considered me quite brave, holding my own during this ordeal. Looking at the bright side, none of my pals ever asked me to help them tidy their rooms.

I love reading books, novels, mysteries, and biographies, anything that catches the imagination. We were on our way north to the hills of Galilee for some mid-course manoeuvres; a three-hour drive. I sat next to the driver, charged with the task of giving directions; not very complicated, as I knew the area pretty well. We stopped for sandwiches, outside the police station in the town of Afula. I was totally engrossed in A. J. Cronin's novel *The Citadel*, which I continued to read avidly throughout lunch and for most of the journey. Twenty minutes or so after leaving

Afula I suddenly realised I'd left my rifle under a tree outside the police station. Any soldier will tell you the potential seriousness of such a crime. I could only think of a court martial, of being disgraced and thrown off the course. Luck was on my side though. I persuaded the driver to return with me, on the pretext that we had to obtain special permits for our manoeuvres from the local police. Believe it or not, the rifle was still there, quietly resting in the shade of the tree. When we finally arrived back, an irritated company captain demanded to know where the hell I had been. 'We seem to have taken the long way round, a sort of scenic route,' I responded. It probably lost me several marks for poor map-reading but I was able to finish the course. My overall performance wasn't as disastrous as I'd anticipated. I finished with a B, and that mainly because of my lack of discipline; not paying attention to orders, general untidiness and the inability to create a shiny mirror on shoes.

Three months of national service remained, so I took the odd decision to volunteer to join the paratroopers. The course itself proved far harder physically than the eventual jumps from the aircraft. Throwing yourself off high scaffolding, knowing that the straps will cut into your thighs just before you land isn't something you'd look forward to. Nevertheless, I doubt whether anyone that has ever parachuted forgets their first jump.

I recall waiting in line, heart thumping as I edged closer and closer to the exit. Despite the tension, I couldn't help noticing a rather pretty, short and slender female disappearing through the hatch without hesitation. The next soldier directly in front of me, a captain, was suddenly hit by a bout of the 'frights', and was unceremoniously pushed out. Suddenly it was my turn. I certainly wasn't going to give anyone the pleasure of shoving me out. That split second, as you look down to the ground a million miles away and step out into nothing, is an anxious and frightening moment, whatever anybody says or claims to the contrary. You're all alone, you and yourself, a tiny speck in the middle of an infinite universe. As the parachute opened I was instantly engulfed by a shroud of silence. Any semblance of tension, fear and anxiety evaporated into the surrounding thin air. I looked around and realised that everyone was shouting and laughing out of sheer relief. In the middle of the descent I passed the young girl, clearly my male instincts had not deserted me; she was obviously somewhat lighter than I. Far more seriously however, was the fact that the ground seemed to be approaching at an alarming speed. Just in time, I crouched, landed and ran around the parachute as instructed to ensure not to be dragged along the sand. Looking around, I became aware that the girl – who turned out to be a doctor – having landed just behind me, hadn't had time to complete the manoeuvre and was consequently being blown past me. I quickly grabbed her by the feet and held on for dear life. We gradually slowed down and were able to complete the proper final release operation. It was the nearest I ever got to her!

But I did meet my first girlfriend when still a paratrooper. Early on we were shown around the camp, with special attention being paid to the section where the parachutes were folded, presumably to give us a sense of confidence at the meticulous safety standards being maintained. I started to talk to one of the girls, Judith, who, it turned out, lived in a kibbutz not far from Merchavya. After many debates with my soul, my shadow, and myself, I looked her up after my first jump, very proud that I had survived and, most importantly, had not been pushed but had stepped out of the plane of my own volition.

She was slightly built, with lovely dark brown eyes that looked straight at you – no coyness there. She had a head of beautiful black, curly hair. She was of Dutch descent but her mannerisms and attitudes were truly Israeli. The world was either white or black, with no shady areas, a view of life I really wasn't ready or able to cope with. While it lasted though, it proved a wonderful period, giving me a sense of wellbeing. A member of the opposite sex was prepared to go out with me – what an achievement! Why this should have bothered me at the venerable age of twenty-one is difficult to explain but I certainly enjoyed her company. You knew exactly where you stood with her while I, on the other hand, hummed and hawed, a truly late developer in that department.

During those two-and-a-half years in the army, there wasn't a great deal of communication with my family in Israel or abroad. My priority was survival — physical, mental and emotional. Aunt Irene began mending fences by sending me a home-knitted jumper. I never told her it was practically twice my size, but it gave me great comfort to know that she thought of — and cared for — me. After that our relationship prospered, never flagging even though Dolphie's attitude toward me remained cold and frosty to the very end.

My brother Jacques, who had in the meantime emigrated to Australia, was by now divorced with two children. He came to visit me in Israel en route to Europe. It was just at the period I was heavily engaged crawling through the sands of the Negev, weighed down with a full army pack. Knowing the machinations of the military, he managed to get me a three-day pass and a much-appreciated respite from military exercises. Boy, was I grateful to my eldest brother!

Meanwhile, Ossie and Trudy had become the proud parents of three young sons. Although I was vaguely aware that financially matters were pretty tough for them, no mention was ever made of any health problems. I did, of course, also maintain contact with Emilie, my foster mother. This tended to take the form of postcards. The limited space meant I could be brief and not indulge in long explanations of my ever-changing lifestyles, the communal kibbutz system or life in the Israeli Army which would have been so alien to her. Anyway, my fluency in German was fast evaporating.

It was a wonderful feeling to collect my demobilisation papers, shove everything into a kit bag and walk away from camp in civilian clothes. On closer inspection of the papers, I realised that I was already going to be called up for reserve duty in September, just five months away. Call-up and reserve duties were, and still are, an integral part of Israeli life.

On returning home to Merchavya, I was put on kitchen duty, which involved washing hundreds of plates and innumerable pieces of cutlery, night after night for three months. I began to imagine what a dish-washing robot would feel like. Then there were the night patrols; wandering around the perimeter fence of the kibbutz, trying desperately to stay awake by visualising dark, shadowy figures lurking behind every tree. I even managed a few, brief visits to Judith, which were not enhanced by having either to hitch or, worse still, trek for a couple of hours in the middle of the night, before the start of some ungodly early morning shift.

Eventually, it was agreed that I should teach English in the lower school from the start of the new school year, in September. This was undoubtedly going to be a challenge. How was I going to teach an uninhibited, rowdy bunch of children to understand, even if only in a limited way, the nuances of the English language? I decided to organise games and then give the kids short tests; something they were not used to, and somewhat contrary to the kibbutz educational ethos.

Amazingly it worked. Every lesson I returned the papers with comments, which were discussed in class before starting a different game, song or quiz. We were just beginning to enjoy our mutual communication, increasingly using English vocabulary when the reminder for my first army reserve call-up arrived. It was supposed to have lasted three weeks, but in the event, I didn't return home for a couple of months.

The initial reserve exercises passed without hitch. Exactly why I spent days cooped up in a rubber dinghy learning to navigate this mini floating vessel between merchant ships docked in the port of Haifa I never could fathom. On completion of this rather unusual course we were allocated a bus to take us back to our various homes.

En route, the driver stopped at a petrol station to refuel. As he was filling up, the phone rang. Unbelievably, it was an order to return to camp. A pretty poor joke. Or so we thought. But it was nothing of the kind. On arriving, there was barely time to dismount before being given precise instructions for the special duties we were about to undertake. Imagine my surprise to discover I'd become a communications officer. What did I know of those cumbersome walky-talkies I'd seen other soldiers lugging around. As I was being hustled toward a Piper plane, waiting to take off, I was informed that I was to make contact with the brigade that had just jumped onto the slopes of the Mitla Pass, in the middle of the Sinai Desert. This was the first I had heard that there was to be a Sinai campaign, never mind that it was already well underway. It was November 1956 and Israel was at war over the Suez Canal.

'Your pilot is an experienced navigator so you shouldn't have too many problems,' I was advised. That proved a rather inaccurate statement.

'And who am I communicating with?' I queried.

'The Boss, Arik Sharon,' was the curt response.

By then, Sharon was already a pretty well-known character; impetuous, brave and someone who didn't suffer fools gladly. His orders had to be obeyed immediately and if possible before he barked them out. Otherwise you'd probably find yourself the recipient of one of his usual, torrid tongue-lashings. Orders he was given, on the other hand, could be disregarded if he didn't believe them to be correct. As far as he was concerned, plans he was provided with were merely guidelines to be improved on, as and how he deemed necessary. A sort of Israeli malaise: 'I can do anything better than you, and *I* am always right'.

Looking at Sharon's history, it's quite revealing how, time and again, his actions, or those he participated in, caused high numbers of casualties. From as far back as the attack on Qibya in 1953, through the Sinai Campaign in 1956, the Yom Kippur War, the Lebanon debacle and the more recent years of the Palestinian uprising. These were predominantly retaliatory actions but the cost in human terms, and subsequent anguish on both sides, proved devastating. Having said that, to cast him as the all-time villain shows a lack of insight and of understanding as to the make-up of the original pioneers, and their first-generation offspring. The generation Sharon grew up with – Ben Gurion, the first prime minister of Israel; Moshe Dayan, Israel's most famous chief-of-staff; Golda Meir, the first female prime minister in the western world – surely shared some common links that went beyond the immediate security issues. The strongest and the one that springs instantly to mind is, of course, generic to all Israelis of that period. Having just escaped the dark, murky fog of the pogroms in Eastern Europe, and the even more devastating effects of the Holocaust, where millions of Jews were taken to the gas chambers showing little resistance, it was essential to prove that Israel was not about to passively go the same way. A further close tie was the Bible, which graphically describes the numerous battles for freedom and survival that the Children of Israel were forced to fight and which virtually became a way of life. The Old Testament is littered with wars that go as far back as Jacob, Joseph, Moses, Joshua, and David, then via Massada, Bar Kochba and Judas Maccabbias through to our own more recent generations – invariably the issue is one of fighting for survival.

These first settlers, and their children, were determined at all costs not to let history repeat itself. Consequently, as time went on, 'an eye for an eye' became 'two eyes for an eye' and it appears an ever-present chord since the creation of the State of Israel in 1948. Ironically, it's this tunnel vision, however understandable, which could, in the long run, endanger the achievements of the original pioneers. It somehow obscures the fact that the Canaanites, the Phoenicians and the Philistines all lived in, and inhabited this region at about the same time as the Hebrews. A long history of conflict between all the parties involved is one that is unlikely to be resolved by force.

Maybe we should remind ourselves that as intelligent human beings we are capable of communicating through the spoken word and should be able to find compromises in order to resolve issues, rather than resorting primarily to physical confrontation. As usual there are, of course, two sides to the conflict and without both sides agreeing to talk and compromise the stalemate will, no doubt, remain, with all its inherent dangers.

Back to the Piper plane patiently waiting to whisk me off across the Sinai desert. I must confess, the pilot seemed a pretty laid-back individual as he patiently explained how to buckle up and use the radio monitor. By the time we took off into the dark skies, I couldn't help pondering, *What next?* In fact, I wasn't even sure how the communication link was going to work. I needn't have worried though –

we were hardly above the clouds when the radio crackled into life and a rasping voice came through loud and clear.

'Where the hell are you?'

'On our way,' I replied. Talk about being impatient. In that department, I would say Sharon took all the honours. It must have been about an hour or so later, just as I was becoming a little anxious, that I noticed bright lights looming up ahead.

'We've flown too far,' I pointed out to the pilot. 'In fact,' I continued, 'we're about to cross the Suez Canal.'

Maybe the Egyptians weren't yet aware that Israeli paratroopers had landed in the Sinai.

We made a sharp U-turn in a northerly direction and, after numerous one-sided radio conversations, we finally made contact with the battalion at the Mitla Pass and landed beside them. There, we learned of the casualties suffered by our paratroopers when ambushed by the Egyptians the previous day. I still remember the hill we crawled up to find out how they were faring after the jump and subsequent fighting – most seemed tired but in pretty good shape. Having achieved our goal, it was time to communicate with the armoured regiment on its way to Mitla. Our orders were pretty clear: 'Get back on the plane and return to base, now!'

We said our goodbyes and couldn't have been more than about fifty metres from the plane when suddenly two Egyptian aircraft came screaming across the sky toward us. Everyone ducked behind rocks, bushes or anything that appeared vaguely like shelter. A couple of seconds later, bullets strafed along the ground, hitting, amongst other things, our poor little Piper, which promptly, as if in utter anguish, burst into flames. My immediate concern wasn't how close a shave that was but how strong the Boss's curses were going to be for not having departed earlier.

There weren't many options open to us. We stayed put, and waited for the armoured division to catch up. At that point, my assignment and role as communications officer had been completed, if a little ahead of schedule, so I become a platoon leader and part of the infantry making its way south towards the Canal. Most of the camps we passed were empty, littered mainly with clothes, boots and huge piles of halva, which I can only assume was part of the staple Egyptian diet. We did encounter the odd bit of resistance. During one of these skirmishes I came face to face with an Egyptian soldier, turning toward me and lifting his rifle. I watched it rise, in a kind of slow motion arc, as he prepared to shoot. For an instant, I stood transfixed, rooted to the ground. Then, fumbling with heart pounding, ticking rapidly like an internal time bomb, I aimed my rifle and squeezed the trigger. I have no idea who shot first – evidently, even if the Egyptian soldier did, he missed. Luckily for me, I didn't.

I have never managed to erase that moment, even though it took place sixty years ago. For months, I couldn't help wondering who he was, what his family were like and how they reacted when they discovered he had died in battle. It's quite scary, although I have somehow stifled these qualms for many years, those questions are still there, unanswered. What if he hadn't turned and pointed his rifle at me, or if I had been killed instead of him?

We arrived at what became our final destination, near Sharm el-Sheikh on the Red Sea, just as a hasty cease fire and armistice was declared. Being reservists, we were among the first to be discharged. I had, in the meantime, met up with a couple of my kibbutz friends, who like myself, had decided to use the opportunity to explore an area we weren't sure would be open to Israelis in the future. We borrowed a jeep that seemed superfluous to regiment requirements and headed off toward Mount Sinai.

Looking back, it was a rather dangerous venture. For a start, none of us had a driving licence or could even drive properly. Manoeuvring tractors in the field was the limit of our expertise. Nor were there any maps available to guide us if we took a wrong turning. We needn't have worried; there were no turnings, just a single narrow road gradually deteriorating into a winding dirt track along which we had to drive with extreme care to avoid slipping down the steep embankments on either side. Amazingly, we did remember to fill up with petrol before setting out and, still more miraculously, we didn't get lost. The monks who opened the gate at St Katherine's Monastery must have thought that God had sent three holy ghosts to punish them when they found themselves confronted by three filthy, dust-covered Israeli soldiers armed with STEN guns. After the initial shock, however, they proved very hospitable, showing us around and giving us food and lodgings for the night. They even volunteered a guide for the following day.

The next morning, a 3am start for the first of many climbs I later undertook to Mount Sinai's peak, some 2,300 metres high. It took just over two hours and, as we reached the top, out of breath after climbing up the eight hundred steps or so at the end of our trek, the skies began to brighten, with streaks of light breaking up the fast disappearing dark night. The panoramic views that greeted us from the top were breath-taking. Watching the mist disperse over the mountain range for miles around, I was able, for the first time, to contemplate the possibility of someone standing there alone, in the stillness of dawn, either hearing or imagining voices.

The silence, as the sun rose majestically over the horizon, was at once stunning and eerie. Moses, standing there, a solitary figure, those many centuries ago, couldn't have discovered a better spot to meditate and then produce ten of the most famous sentences of all time. Nor, I suspect, could he have ever envisaged the effect his commandments would have over hundreds of future generations.

We scrambled back down to the monastery for a humble monk's breakfast and, after thanking our surprised hosts for their hospitality, continued our journey of discovery through the Sinai Desert. This is undoubtedly one of the most beautiful and awe-inspiring landscapes in the world. It has acted as a safe haven for Jews, Christians and Muslims alike, on their travels between holy sites, from time immemorial, whether to St Katherine's Monastery, Jerusalem or Mecca. It also provided refuge for those escaping Pharaonic regimes, Babylonian emperors or Assyrian armies creating havoc on their way down from the north.

We didn't linger too long; after all, we had been demobbed and it was time to show our faces at home again. We did still manage to visit the old disused turquoise mines, dating back to the time of the Pharaohs, and clamber through the wonderful coloured canyon. I've been back through this glorious desert many times since, mainly taking either cycling or trekking groups. No matter which way I travel I am always stunned and uplifted by the sheer splendour of the clean air, space and beauty of the Sinai Desert.

After all this, we embarked on a six-hour drive back home with no accidents or any clashes with police. We were back by the end of that week, having survived some pretty awful driving on the way, and with only just about enough petrol in the tank. I have no idea what happened to the jeep which, I ought to mention. It had at one time belonged to the Egyptian army. Most importantly we were greeted like returning heroes. Why, I can't imagine. For us, in our early twenties, it was all about participating in a unique and successful adventure. Even my encounter with death did not diminish the sense of achievement. After this rather exciting interlude, the world of politics began its usual manoeuvring and haggling over how best to resolve the Suez Crisis which, as we now know, intimately involved Britain and France, not, I suspect, to be protective of Israel but looking after their personal interests in the Middle East.

Meanwhile, it was back to routine, in my case teaching English to eleven and twelve-year-olds. Somehow, even in this relatively tranquil world of children's education, I managed to become embroiled in discourses on some kibbutz ethic or other. The teaching fraternity was clearly unhappy that, without asking prior permission, I had decided not only to set the kids a few tests, but also to make comments on their work. Not giving grades, mind you, just pointing out mistakes and noting what I thought of their work. This went against the basic philosophical ideology of self-motivation. The general gist of the fraternity's comments went something like: 'The children may be enjoying your lessons, feel a sense of achievement and have improved their knowledge of English, but we can't return to the old, out-dated capitalist methods, can we now?'

I look at the way things are today, where exams, even on the kibbutz, are virtually the only criteria by which young people's intellectual and academic abilities are judged – and the paths for their future prospects laid – and wonder if there's no middle ground. Does every system have to contain absolutes from which nobody is permitted to deviate? When the ideology fails to deliver and the formula collapses, our children have to go through the upheaval of having to adapt to another similarly intractable system. I have become increasingly sceptical that any of our modern societies have the ability, or the maturity, to search for more pragmatic, germinal approaches to this or any other subject.

Chapter Eight

First return to England, aged 22

By many lands and over many a wave
I come, my brother, to your piteous grave,
To bring you the last offering in death
And o'er dumb dust expend an idle breath;
For fate has torn your living self from me,
Snatched you, brother, Oh, how cruelly!
You take these gifts, as our fathers bade
For sorrow's tribute to the passing shade;
A brother's tears have wet them o'er and o'er;
And so my brother, hail, and farewell ever more!

Catullus

It was a couple of months or so later in early 1957, while on a weekend visit to Auntie Irene in Haifa, that she asked whether I'd like to visit my brother Ossie in England. Of course, I hadn't seen him since coming to Israel eight years earlier. Somewhat surprised, I enquired if anything was wrong.

'Well,' she replied, 'he's in hospital with some kind of skin disease and I thought that after such a long period of army service and fighting wars, you might like a break.'

'Is he seriously ill?'

'Not as far as I'm aware,' she assured me.

Uncle Dolphie's firm owned and leased several small cargo ships, sailing across the Mediterranean to ports in Europe, so travelling to England didn't present a problem.

More difficult was getting leave from the kibbutz. After much discussion, I managed to obtain special dispensation for a few weeks' vacation. Similarly, getting permission to travel abroad for whatever reason was no easy matter. For a start, I had to forfeit a year's annual leave in advance. Then there was the little matter of equality, or rather inequality. Why should I be allowed to travel abroad just because I had relatives who had the means to help? After all there were so many long-standing members who would have loved to have had the opportunity to travel abroad and visit their relatives. I suppose the fact that my brother was ill and in hospital swayed the decision. None of us though was aware of how serious the situation really was.

Naturally, I had to rely on Auntie Irene for the funding of the trip, which she generously supplied. The idea of returning to England for the first time in eight long years – having left there really a child at the tender age of thirteen, and now a young man who had had to grow up very quickly – was exciting. I couldn't wait to visit my brother and his family, as well as see my foster mother in Dorking.

I had always felt an innate close bond to Ossie, maybe due to coming on the Kindertransport together. At just nineteen, Ossie had married Trudy from the East End of London. They were market stall traders at Petticoat Lane and Walthamstow. I had attended their wedding before coming to Israel and somehow, through Auntie and occasional letters to each other, had kept up to date with the birth of their three sons. I was looking forward to the trip very much. It would be a break from the army, the war and the perpetual discussions on the various issues that kibbutz life centred on.

Parting from Judith with whom I had, in the meanwhile, created a friendly and easy-going companionship was bound to hurt. As it turned out, the relationship didn't survive our separation and perhaps it wouldn't have anyway.

Before departing, I was given numerous instructions as to who I should visit en route – a cousin in Lyon, another in Antwerp, a distant relative in Paris – the list was endless. In the event, the only stop I made was in Lyon.

The ship I boarded in Haifa had only one passenger cabin, and was carrying a full load of oranges bound for Genoa and Marseilles. Being the nephew of the owner, I was treated with great respect including dining in the officers' mess. It was all rather different to my arrival at the same port some eight years earlier and no comparison to the facilities I encountered on that trip to Israel. The first part of the journey was uneventful; we didn't even experience the distraction of a bout of bad weather. So, I had to find alternative means of keeping myself amused. Being left to your own devices can often prove a wonderfully enriching experience, even if at times it entails simply staring and watching the waves rise and fall in monotonous rhythm over large expanses of water. I did have plenty of books, most of which I had pinched from my uncle's vast collection of mysteries and thrillers.

The most exciting moments came when passing through the straits of Messina. We sighted in quick succession the two volcanic mountains, Etna and Stromboli, the latter spewing out its usual, thin streaks of steam. It brought to mind not only my original sailing eight years earlier in the opposite direction, but also the eruption of Vesuvius, the junior of the 'terrible three' in AD 79, devastating the city of Pompeii, and I couldn't help but wonder what those horrific moments must have been like just before that lethal cloud of volcanic gas and ash hit the frantic, desperate population trying to flee.

Our arrival in Genoa changed this slow, uneventful, but oh so peaceful pace of life. The serenity of my mind, filled contentedly with the mysteries of Poirot, Marlowe, Maigret and Holmes mixed in a brew with *1984*, *Animal Farm* and *The Grapes of Wrath*, was suddenly shattered by a hive of activity, of cranes and lorries clattering around the side of the ship. Boxes of oranges were quickly lifted and unceremoniously dropped with crashing regularity onto an open vehicle parked alongside the ship. The problem was that, this being Italy, once a lorry disappeared, another didn't arrive for some considerable time. Inevitably, the unloading process seemed to be taking longer than originally planned. It didn't bother me. I was happy being in a new environment, ready for some adventure.

I decided a stroll into town would prove a more interesting prospect than boxes of oranges being dropped onto lorries. A few missed and burst open; producing the sight of oranges rolling all over the quay, most of them ending up in the murky waters of the sea. The parting advice hurled at me by the crew as I left the safe haven of the ship was, 'Be careful, and don't return too late. It's a long walk from the centre and you can't tell what you'll encounter in the middle of the night wandering alone along through these eerie, empty dockyards.' Did I take heed?

It didn't take long to realise what a 'long way' meant. The bus, which operated at irregular times and only during the day, took about half-an-hour to get to the fringes of town. This would entail a lengthy trek back on foot if I missed the last one. Finding a timetable, or somebody who could tell me when the last bus was scheduled, proved an elusive mission. My Italian being non-existent, I reverted to much hand-signalling, which the locals found amusing, a smattering of German, which nobody wanted to understand, and the occasional word in Hebrew, which of course proved totally incomprehensible. Anyway, the immediate priority was to assuage my ever-mounting hunger, never mind local bus schedules. I finally discovered a café where the prices, in the lower thousands of lire, seemed cheap even for the back streets of Genoa, and managed to point out a pasta dish. I obviously liked it being the first of countless pasta dishes I have devoured over the years. It is hard to imagine life without pasta now and to believe that at twenty-two this food was new to me is something my children wouldn't be able to comprehend.

The little I'd read about Genoa before arriving indicated that one of its more interesting sights was the cemetery overlooking the harbour. I'm not sure what morbid fascination led me to make it my first port of call but that is exactly where I headed. Not wishing to go through the whole process of finding the right bus again by means of hand signals, and probably getting lost in the process, I decided to buy a map and walk. The cemetery turned out to be just a short bus ride from the centre of town but I resolved to get there on foot. I convinced myself that walking would give me the opportunity to see some of the bustling narrow back roads, you know, the real Genoa. What I actually passed were numerous butchers, fruit stalls and children kicking balls aimlessly at each other. Hearing the local inhabitants using their lovely melodic Italian vocal chords to the full, as they tried to draw the attention of friends or members of their family half way down the other end of the street, was in itself quite an experience and a taste of the local atmosphere.

The Staglieno Cemetery, created in the mid-nineteenth century, was a revelation, a bit like walking through a beautiful, landscaped, open-air gallery, filled with neo-classical, art nouveau and art deco sculptures and monuments. There were tombs for families with bronze statues of relatives mourning, others for small children, their mothers grieving over the tomb. Although a cemetery is not necessarily the first place you'd consider spending an afternoon, this one is truly exceptional. Some of the mausoleums scattered about are not only works of art but surrounded by the most glorious gardens, generating an atmosphere of quiet serenity, especially in the middle of the week when few tourists are around. On the other hand, there were also quite over-the-top, ugly, monstrous-looking tombstones. I suppose it is difficult to have one without the other. The grounds are vast and, as you climb numerous steps up the hillside, the vistas over the bay and city below expand and open up onto the most wonderful views.

As I stood marvelling at the coastline below, I couldn't help but be reminded of a similar panoramic view when peering from my aunt's balcony on Mount Carmel, in Haifa. One of the graves I visited was that of Oscar Wilde's wife, the prospect of which had attracted me to the cemetery, but it paled into insignificance beside its surroundings. A much later visit to Wilde's tomb in Paris proved a far greater emotional experience, more, I am sure, to do with the personalities involved than the aesthetic beauty of their final resting places.

It was late afternoon by the time I returned to the city centre, where I roamed along the main streets, peering into shops at items priced way beyond my meagre means. I quickly tired and decided a visit to the cinema would while away the time and take my mind off my lack of funds. Being aware that most films were dubbed, I went in search of a possible reprieve and thought I found one in *Annie Get Your Gun*, a musical I deemed impossible to dub. Wrong – only the songs were sung in the original language. I stayed for a while but gave up after watching lip movements totally out of sync with the spoken word.

Unfortunately, by the time I came out of the cinema the last connection to the port had departed so I started off on a long, dark trek. As I approached the port area, I passed a group of what appeared to be middle-aged women, seated on a bench chatting and laughing; in retrospect they were probably no older than their mid-thirties. I'd hardly walked a few steps beyond where they were sitting when a couple of them rose and started following me, gesticulating and waving for me to wait. I suppose they assumed I was a sailor 'in need'. Looking around the deserted quay I decided to beat a hasty retreat toward the ship. They must have been pretty desperate and hard up; why else did they continue to follow me? Fortunately, they gave me up as a lost cause and anyway I could run much faster.

I honestly can't imagine what frightened me, after all what was the worst that could have happened? A lesson in physical promiscuity and the loss of the few lire I had in my pocket? I suppose, never having been confronted in such a manner before, I panicked. Anyway, I wouldn't have proved much of a catch sexually, and certainly not financially. What can I say? There I was, a young man in his early-twenties, after military service and a war, oblivious of the world some inhabit and now discovering how others were obliged to live, in order to survive. I arrived back at the ship pretty late to be informed that the crew had been about to send a search party out for me. Unbelievably, the unloading had been completed earlier than planned and we were sailing at dawn. I was far too embarrassed to tell anyone about my late evening encounter with the 'girls', and my ignominious retreat.

We arrived in Marseilles the following day leaving behind a rather comfortable week where everything was done for me and with no responsibilities other than eating, avidly reading, sleeping or wandering aimlessly along the deck. It was time to work out how I was going to make my way to London, with a short stopover in Lyon. My French, only marginally better than my Italian, was of little help. Nor could I remember much from the visit to Marseilles on my way to Israel those many years before. At least the Italians are prepared to listen and try to help a stranger in distress. The same can't be said for the inhabitants of Marseilles, whose way of getting rid of you is to wave their arms in the general direction you should head and then promptly disappear. Eventually, I located the main railway station and somehow managed to work out the departure times for Lyon.

Although I spent a couple of nights at my cousin's house in one of the outer suburbs, I remember little except that my cousin was a pretty large and heavily-built individual; not at all like his brother Eliezer in Merchavya.

Impressively, the night train from Lyon entered the station in Paris exactly on schedule. In Paris, I met up with the daughter of my cousin Eliezer, as we were both briefly there. I then made my way by train, ship and train again to London, finally arriving at Victoria Station a day or two later. My first problem on arriving in London was to discover the best way of getting to Ossie and Trudy's home, somewhere in Walthamstow, east London. I asked a policeman standing near the buses parked outside the station. Trying to be helpful he suggested that the way to reach my destination was to take a bus to Camden Town then change and continue on the 253 the rest of the way. I took his advice. An hour later I found out that a third bus, the 38, was required to take me down Lea Bridge Road. To add insult to injury I then discovered that had I boarded the 38 double decker standing at Victoria station I could have shortened the journey by at least an hour, travelling without any changes! I have never asked direction from a policeman since.

As I approached Ossie and Trudy's home, I wondered whether they had changed much, or would recognise me. More importantly, how would I relate to the nephews I had never met and who didn't know me? I was about to knock, when I spotted a note pinned to the door, directing me to their neighbours. The next few moments pierced my core, an instant nightmare I desperately hoped to wake up from and discover that it was all indeed just a bad dream. A split second in life that remains with you forever. My brother had passed away. Youth's resistance to body blows and emotional shocks somehow evaporate with each passing year. As a child there is no end, just a future filled with discovery and anticipation. When maturity sets in, apprehension somehow displaces the hope we all harbour during those naïve growing-up years. I seemed to have coped far better at the age of twelve learning my foster father had suddenly passed away than finding out, again quite unexpectedly, that my brother had died just two days before my arrival. Despite being twenty-two and a war veteran hardened by army service, the impact really was traumatic. I stood transfixed, not able to take in or believe that Ossie, my twenty-seven-year-old brother, who I had come to visit, wasn't there any more, indeed was already buried in a Jewish cemetery in East London.

Trudy and the boys were sitting Shiva, the ancient Jewish custom of mourning for seven days in the company of close family and friends, at an aunt's in Northwest London. As I made my way towards Golders Green, where the family was grieving, I sensed that the journey ahead was going to prove long and arduous. I would always feel a sense of regret that I didn't arrive before his death, and that I wasn't there for him and Trudy, even if only for a short part of his last agonising period. Being told later that Ossie was aware of my imminent arrival and so much looking forward to seeing his 'baby brother' simply upsets me every time my mind returns to the terrible sadness of that moment.

Why, oh why didn't anybody tell me how seriously ill he was? Ossie had apparently not enjoyed good health as a child but I had no idea. They all knew and had even consulted my Uncle Bobby, another of my mother's brothers, who was a doctor in the States, but who had advised that there was little hope. Back in the Fifties one didn't talk about cancer – it was regarded as a disease you simply shouldn't be afflicted with, a bit like AIDS in later generations.

As I entered the room, it took me several minutes to digest the heart rending picture of Trudy sitting surrounded by her three little boys – the youngest, Lawrence, was barely two and like me, was to grow up with no memory of his father. A family deprived of a husband and father who had survived the Holocaust but succumbed to the ravages of cancer. The reason for my coming had changed dramatically; there was now no question of staying for just a few weeks. The family needed help and, whilst I was in no position to provide financial assistance, I could at least be of use giving emotional support. Initially it was simply a case of being there during the last days of the Shiva, then helping Ossie's family get their lives back to some normality by staying in the house for a while.

However unbearable, Trudy somehow managed to find life after the loss of her husband, at so young an age, and with the responsibility of bringing up three young boys on her own. She bore up to the task wonderfully well. Of course, there were periods of depression, anguish and unabated floods of tears but these tended to be swallowed and held back during the day when the children needed attending to. Relative youth, I suppose, helped absorb some of the pain. I hope and believe that my being close at hand during that sad period was of some comfort to her.

It was time to plan the immediate future – how to survive with no money and a visa clearly stipulating that I was not allowed to enter paid employment. The solution came in the form of youth work for the kibbutz movement. In reality, this constituted a sort of brain-washing of Jewish youngsters, promoting the idea that their destiny lay in emigrating to Israel in order to help settle the country by living and working in one of the communal agricultural settlements scattered across the land. The 1950s was a period of emotional instability in the Jewish communities, a time when only some of the torrid details of the Holocaust had begun to dribble into the public consciousness. The various Jewish youth movements of the time – Hashomer Hatzair; The Young Guard, the most radically left and the one I belonged to; Habonim, The Builders; and Bnai Akiva, The Sons of the Prophet Akiva, the most religious – were fertile ground for persuading many Anglo-Jewish youths to take the plunge and emigrate to the newly-formed Jewish State of Israel.

These movements were a sort of a hybrid of a youth club – offering indoor and outdoor activities – and a young person's socio-political movement where heated debates around the political issues of the day took place. In our case the discussions tended to revolve around 'Liberating Socialism' versus 'Oppressive Imperialism'. Suddenly, I had become an emissary for the Hashomer Hatzair kibbutz movement. What did I know of organising activities for groups of youngsters, or arranging summer camps in exotic locations such as the slopes of Snowdon? Never mind ensuring back-up plans in case of evacuation from washed out, muddy fields in North Wales, an annual occurrence in that part of the world.

I became an expert in local school accommodation, and regulations governing the use of such institutions. Believe me, there were plenty, even then. We had a training farm, Dowar House, not far from Bishops Stortford in Essex where, over the following couple of years, I made my home for periods of time. It was here the prospective young emigrants (*Chalutzim* in Hebrew), wishing to live on a kibbutz, spent several months working on the land before making the final move. It was very similar to the farm in Thaxted where I'd spent a few weeks before leaving for Israel in 1949. Except, at that time I was only thirteen. Most of those living at the Dower House Farm were in their late teens and early twenties. They were there for ideological reasons. In Thaxted, I was a young boy running between one kind of life and another. Here I was a young adult trying to persuade other youngsters that a move to a kibbutz in Israel was a far more worthwhile and potentially satisfying life than remaining in England.

Getting everyone up in the dark, early hours on a winter's morning wasn't my idea of pleasure, but all in all it wasn't a bad way of life and we experienced plenty of rather exciting moments. Like for example when one of the boys took a dislike to a particular female resident and, after a heated argument, decided to throw all her belongings out of the first-floor window, onto the muddy ground below. There followed a very serious group therapy session, which finished several hours later with both parties agreeing to make up, even though they probably disliked each other more vehemently than before. I suspect none of the rest of us was any the wiser as to what caused the friction in the first place. My therapy was to take a book and go to bed, on the basis that everything looks brighter in the morning after a decent night's sleep. In reality, it took several nights of deep slumber to reduce their mutual animosity to manageable proportions.

Apart from my role at Dower House, I also helped run the youth club in Nightingale Road, Clapton, set on the fringes of the old Jewish East End. The problem was that trying to maintain this kind of schedule by public transport proved virtually impossible. One of the members, Tuvia, came up with the bright idea of getting a motorbike. I'd be able to ride with L-plates and wouldn't require a valid driving licence, which I didn't possess. A Liverpudlian, and an apparent font of mechanical and vehicular knowledge, Tuvia volunteered to drive us up to Liverpool in the farm van where he knew of a fantastic second-hand motorbike shop. Patently we hadn't thought the matter through properly. Why on earth traipse all the way to Liverpool when you could probably purchase the same item at a similar price in London? I suppose the very mention of a 'deal' creates a kind of smoke screen obliterating normal mental faculties. In Tuvia's case the ulterior motive was a free trip home and the prospect of his first decent meal in months. He lost out on both counts.

After travelling for nearly five hours, and just as we were entering the outskirts of Liverpool, Tuvia suddenly exclaimed, 'Shit! I forgot - it's Yom Kippur.' Luckily the motorbike shop-owner wasn't Jewish so we managed to buy a small, rather insignificant-looking bike, loaded it onto the back of the van and sadly, given Tuvia's parents were fasting, started making our way back south without the anticipated visit or much-needed decent meal. Tuvia just couldn't bring himself to confront his parents and tell them that he had driven all the way to Liverpool on Yom Kippur, and that he was starving.

The motorbike and I had quite a few 'bonding' experiences. Our first such encounter happened soon after returning to Dower House. Having listened carefully to copious instructions on how to manoeuvre the bike and what to avoid I set out on my very first ride. The roads around the area had little traffic, on the other hand most were narrow winding country lanes. The initial couple of hundred yards were navigated with consummate ease. It was the first bend that caused trouble. I steered the bike in the right direction but forgot to turn with it, so found myself hurtling over a bush whilst the vehicle continued on the road before careering into a hedge. I stayed out late that day trying desperately to master the art of motorcycling without the ignominy of falling off. It took a little time but eventually I overcame my ultra-cautious approach and, whilst never a 'biker' in the true sense, I did eventually cover many miles on my new friend.

On one occasion, making my way to the youth club on a summer's evening, a police car stopped me on the Lea Bridge Road. *What now?* I thought. 'Excuse me, sir,' a very polite policeman said. 'I believe your brakes need attention.' Quite right – you could hear them screeching a mile away which was of course why he'd stopped me. I assured him that in fact I was on my way to do just that.

Amazingly, despite it being a Sunday when most garages are closed, he bade me farewell and drove off without a warning; not even asking to see my driving licence.

On another occasion, I decided a diversion was required, so I took myself off on my beloved motorbike and hurtled through Richmond Park and along the A24 to Dorking. On arriving, I discovered the town looked much smaller than I had remembered. I suppose everything does when seen through adult eyes, rather than naïve, childhood ones. Emilie had by then moved to stay with her youngest grandchild, Ida, who took wonderful care of her. She suffered from deteriorating lumbago, which meant ever-increasing immobility. It never seemed to affect her positive outlook on life, though. On top of this, her daughter-in-law had died of cancer a few years back, still only in her early forties. Her son Rudl died a year later of what the doctors described as a broken heart. She rarely saw her second son who lived in Germany where he had remained during the entire war, part of which he'd served as a German soldier. Such are the ironies of life.

Emilie was so happy to see me, her nomadic foster son, though sad of course to hear about Ossie whom she'd met a few times. Ida hardly remembered me, or I her, but that really didn't matter as we sat reminiscing over many cups of tea, accompanied by wonderful home-baked cakes. Our main collective memories seemed to revolve around my numerous mishaps and misdeeds. It was just the most wonderful, uplifting few hours, spent chatting about the past, a bit in English and a lot in German. Proof again that those years spent growing up amidst this warm, caring and loving family established the foundations upon which I was able to build a life.

Before returning to London, I thought it might be interesting to visit my old school. *Who knows, there might just be a few of the old teachers still around?* As I walked hesitantly through the main front gate I had to remind myself that I was an adult, not a junior barred from entering this hallowed entrance. I had just stepped into the school building when who should be coming towards me but Mr Jones, the headmaster. For a moment, I stood dumbfounded – old habits die hard. He peered at me and then quick as a flash,

'Reich! I remember you – didn't I give you the cane at least three times?'

'Yes Sir!' I replied, nearly extending my hand for a fourth.

'It seemed to me you spent more time outside my office than in the classroom,' he added.

So somebody did remember me. It turned out that this was his last year before retiring. To be fair to Mr Jones, the feared headmaster, he also recalled my winning the junior cross-country, and even asked a few questions about Israel. As I sped homeward that evening, perched on my motorbike, the cold wind scraping against my face, I couldn't help but feel the inner warmth generated by the brief visit back to my childhood in Dorking.

The pattern of my life took several more twists, presenting me with problems I hadn't encountered before. Undoubtedly, I didn't handle these too well and, as a result, sank into a number of low emotional states I'd never imagined existed. Not having experienced normal family life during most of my formative years, patently affected the way I handled issues that others would probably have taken in their stride. My internal mental make-up is highly strung, to the point of frequently having to overcome self-inflicted spasms of insecurity. The fear of losing yet another human being I had become emotionally involved with seemed to spark and create an overwhelming need to over-compensate; more often than not, unfortunately, producing the opposite reaction to the one intended.

Chapter Nine

London – Israel – London – Israel, aged 22-23

Like one, that on a lonesome road
Doth walk in fear and dread,
And having once turned round walks on,
And turns no more his head;
Because he knows, a frightful fiend
Doth close behind him tread.

Coleridge, The Rime of the Ancient Mariner

Staying on in London I found myself immersed in various different activities: travelling back and forth to the Dower House Farm, arranging events for the youth club, preparing discussion topics and at the same time trying to earn subsistence money by teaching English to foreign students; anything to keep me busy and put to the back of my mind the pain of so unexpectedly losing my brother.

I was constantly aware that Trudy and the boys needed support and so tried to visit them as frequently as possible. Seeing her taut, sad face and looking into her eyes stripped of any sparkle was a reminder of how difficult life can be. At times I felt totally helpless, unable to truly console her and be of real comfort, with a sense of overwhelming inadequacy. The best I could do was to play with the boys and discover that I was able to distract Trudy, even if only for short periods, from her anguish and sorrow. Coming to terms emotionally with my brother's death proved a deep mental challenge.

At twenty-two, one doesn't really grasp the true significance of, or link between, current and past traumatic experiences. The irony, for example, of Ossie escaping the horrors of the Holocaust, losing his parents as a child, and then dying at the young age of twenty-seven from the ravages of cancer, never occurred to me then. At that precise moment, all that mattered was overcoming another personal hurdle and pushing into the background a further set-back. The connection hit me much later, at a stage in life when I began to reflect on what I could or should have achieved and the obstacles that had to be overcome simply to survive. Maybe difficult early experiences should be viewed as a preparation for stumbling blocks we'll probably be confronted with in later life.

Keeping fully occupied with basic day-to-day issues took over, providing a self-protective mechanism. As with previous setbacks it was a matter of trying to comprehend what was happening and getting on with life. It allowed me to mask the need to share deep-rooted anxieties with others, a characteristic that has dogged me since early childhood. Living in an environment with no close friends or family around brought my predicament into sharp relief. Even if I could have summoned the courage to pour out my emotional burdens to somebody there was nobody around with whom I had a close enough relationship to do so. Some of the loneliest moments were during late evenings, cooped up in a small bed-sit somewhere in the depths of 'salubrious' Stroud Green. Those endless hours in the still of the night when time stops and you begin to wonder, not for the first time, how it will all end and who else will disappear from your life. All rather melancholy and sombre, but by morning – with the rain, fog, snow or sun – the urgent problems of the day once again took over. For a while at least, the over-hanging shrouds of mist and uncertainty evaporated. Juggling my timetable to incorporate all the projects I'd promised to undertake between sunrise and midnight, became the overriding priority.

I took David, my eldest nephew, to Dower House. A trip he appeared to enjoy no end. To be let loose on a farm is every young child's dream. Never mind the mud, the grotty food and untidy house. For a youngster, to have space and freedom to roam around was much more important. The *Bayit* ('home' in Hebrew), the house in London in which the youth club activities took place, was located in Nightingale Rd, Clapton; wedged between Stamford Hill, not quite as ultra- religious then as it has become today, and central Hackney, one of the early stomping grounds of the original East End Jews.

Not surprisingly, a decade or so after the end of the Second World War, with the ramifications of the Holocaust still keenly felt, a youth movement offering a new kind of Jewish identity, with an ultimately positive pioneering purpose, attracted many Jewish youngsters from the surrounding area. Well-known local grammar schools, such as Grocers and Skinners, provided fertile minds and the meetings were of an extraordinary intellectual level. Imagine a youth club today where fifteen- and sixteen-year-old teenagers listen and discuss the attributes of Mahler's music or try to make sense of Karl Marx's *Das Kapital*;

where smoking and alcohol are prohibited no matter what age, and the primary objective is the abolition of decadence and a life dedicated to improving society in general and the working classes in particular.

I've recently been party to numerous discussions on the positive effects or otherwise that the youth movement had on us as youngsters. Most experiences, providing they're not emotionally or physically cruel, tend, in my view, to have beneficial elements. During the late 50s and early 60s there was an urgent need to come to terms with one of the most devastating episodes in a people's history. Many nations have had to overcome disasters, whether human-created tragedies or those resulting from natural disasters. Few, if any, have been confronted with anything on the scale of the Holocaust which was heaped on Jewish communities across Europe.

Zionist youth movements in Central and Eastern Europe were already thriving and migration from anti-Semitism to a Jewish safe haven in Palestine was already well under way when the Second World War broke out. In the UK, as stories of the suffering of fellow Jews in the camps filtered into British Jewish consciousness, the youth movement here reacted. The youth organisations provided intellectual stimulus to discuss not only recent events but also to delve into centuries of Jewish trials and tribulations. Most parents were hard pressed trying to make a decent living, never mind discussing politics or analysing the intricate history of the Jews. Many youngsters ended up leaving home much earlier than they would have done, and several delayed their higher education by a few years. Nevertheless, on balance, and without wishing to generalise, I would say it was a price well worth paying.

As a member of a kibbutz, I was considered an expert on the ideology and practice of communism. It was up to me to convey to the young members of the movement that the kibbutz system was the remedy for all evil and the great hope for humanity's glorious future. In hindsight, one can but marvel at the naivety of the young, including myself, where everything is so simple with nothing to distinguish the demarcation lines of deepest black and purest white. The grey of everyday life and the battle for survival just didn't exist. I suppose that since time immemorial, for most young generations, everything is clearly defined as either right or wrong with nothing in between. The experiences we encounter whilst slowly maturing prove, to most of us, that life is not quite as simple as that.

Many of our discussions revolved around the fundamental principles behind the very existence of the kibbutz movement and the apparent link with the philosophy underpinning the Soviet socialist movement. While the latter certainly spoke of relieving the masses of their burdens of inequality and of the destruction of capitalism, at the forefront remained the proclamation that the only way to free the working classes was to embrace a communist proletariat dictatorship. Both of these new creative ideas of egalitarian ways of life thrived before and after World War Two; initially, in the wake of the pogroms at the turn of the century and the Russian Revolution and later greatly reinforced by the inextricable rise of the Nazi regime and its terrible impact on the Jewish people.

There was abundant material to fuel lively debate, particularly as among the main kibbutz principles were voluntary democratic participation, debate and freedom of choice. The only real similarity between the Russian Socialist kolkhoz and the kibbutz was that both were based on a new communal agrarian lifestyle. Thereafter they followed very different patterns. At the time, however, there was a rather romantic tendency to link them together. The kibbutz system, being a Jewish one, deemed it essential to seek numerous justifications and to have endless debates on how best to implement its ideals. Inevitably, you were never quite sure which political line to take or where you stood in the overall scheme of socialist ideology. I'm unlikely to forget the number of times I stood, dressed in the blue uniform of the Hashomer Hatzair (the 'young guard') singing either the Israeli national anthem or the Song of the International Workers, frequently one after the other. Ironically, the lyrics of both were filled with similar symbols of hope, freedom and longing, a sort of nationalistic internationalism.

I suppose I must have done a pretty good job at the time. Many of the youngsters found their way to Israel and a kibbutz even if, in most cases, the adventure proved rather short-lived. Still, we had periods of great fun; camping in muddy fields, playing 'wide games', where the objective was for Israelis and Arabs to ambush each other in the middle of the night. I usually tried to engineer the result as a draw. Of course, this meant nobody was satisfied and the nuances of the rules would get discussed vehemently till the early hours of the morning. Quite why it was called a 'wide game' remains a mystery to me.

Some of the quietest moments during this period were those spent walking home at night through a thick blanket of yellow smog, which seemed to engulf and swallow every moving thing in its wake. It was in marked contrast to the lively debates concerning crucial issues such as 'Should girls be allowed to wear make-up?' and learning the steps of Israeli folk dances, usually accompanied by a member playing the accordion. At times, when that eerie feeling of being the only living soul on earth became overpowering, my mind started playing peculiar tricks. I found it both exhilarating and frightening when, deep in thought, a sense of isolation slowly crept into my psyche, releasing into orbit vivid thoughts of mystical beings, unconsummated longings or even, at times, death. At this point, every step appeared to invite unknown dangers and mysteries that, needless to say, never materialised.

Despite wandering late at night in a fairly run-down area, with visibility virtually non-existent, I was less concerned for my safety than I am today, partially, no doubt, due to youth but also because, despite having just emerged from a horrendous war, somehow the world seemed a much safer place than it does today. The clanging of the trams and the drone of the trolley buses exuded a sense of security; knowing that at any time you could hop on to one before it slowly disappeared into the murky mist ahead.

That summer I took a party of Jewish university undergraduates to Israel for work experience on a kibbutz. It turned out to be an interesting trip. First, en route to Munich by train, I discovered that a member of the group, a rather talkative, vivacious, good looking, young girl in her mid-twenties turned out to be the violinist Nathan Milstein's niece. We had quite an interesting conversation, particularly about her uncle. I'm always intrigued, and not a little envious of those who can play a musical instrument to such a high standard and with sublime ease. A good omen, I thought, especially as at one point she fell asleep with her head on my shoulder. That's as good as it got unfortunately.

We arrived in Munich with some five hours to spare before our connection to Athens so took a short saunter through the city where Hitler had first made his name. I couldn't stop a tremor of angst shaking me as I peered up toward the balcony from where he'd made his infamous speech in the spring of 1923 when, amongst other notorious statements, he pronounced, '...and in this turbulent mass of the workers, the Jew recognised a new power which might perhaps be his instrument for the gaining of that which is his ultimate goal: world supremacy and the destruction of the national states...' I tried to visualise the crowds standing more or less where I stood, absorbing this stream of hatred that poured down over them. I couldn't help but wonder how the masses gathered there could cheer and bask in the glory of Hitler's evil and fanatical outpouring. The possible consequences, if Hitler ever came to power, must already have been apparent to all that were prepared to take note.

We returned to the station well in time to board our connecting train only to discover the place teeming with Greeks on their way home for the summer. It was chaos. The platform was so crowded that the fact we had reserved seats was of little consequence. It was virtually impossible to get on the train. We started pushing members of the group into the appropriate carriage and were doing quite well, or so we thought, until suddenly the train started to move off, on its way to Athens. It wasn't a happy scene for me, the group leader, left on the platform with half the group, the other half hurtling through Germany on their way to Greece. Awful thoughts flashed through my mind of me trying to explain to doting Jewish parents that I'd managed to lose their precious children somewhere between Germany, Austria and Greece.

Luckily common sense prevailed pretty quickly. With an air of indignation and not a little bravado, I marched up to the stationmaster and, in the language I hadn't spoken for several years, began to tell him what I thought of Germany and its railway system in general and Munich Station in particular. Luckily for both of us my German curses were of the childish variety, on top of which I had to delve deep into my memory bank for many of the words I was trying to say. What I eventually managed to blurt out wasn't nearly as bad as I would have liked to utter at that moment. Initially, I must confess, looking into the eyes of that stationmaster, with his peaked hat perched tidily on his head and the groomed suit he was wearing, wasn't a pleasant experience. It was too close in time to the events of the war.

He was most apologetic and tried to console me by explaining that this happened every summer when the Greek workers returned home for their holidays. He also came up with an immediate solution. There was another train due to leave at midnight which would, in all likelihood, be half-empty. More importantly, it would still get us to Athens in time to catch our ship to Israel. Meanwhile, he told me he'd inform the stationmaster at Salzburg to take the other half of the group off the already departed train and tell them to wait for us there. All ended well but I definitely went through hell until we met up again in Salzburg. The rest of the journey proved a doddle by comparison.

I had originally left Israel for three weeks but here I was back after more than a year. It felt good. Nobody in the group fell ill – except those who skived off work on the kibbutz when the going got a bit tough or the weather too hot, or if we had to get up particularly early in the morning. I'm not sure if many made their way back to Israel after graduating but I do know that all of them remembered the experience for many years.

While back in Israel it was, however, agreed that after seeing the group back to England I should stay and continue my youth work in the UK for another year. I too felt I needed more time to help Trudy and the boys so I was happy with that decision.

It was after I'd returned, and as the autumn days began to shorten, that I started accompanying one of the girls from the Youth Club home. Yona lived in the opposite direction to my digs. I suppose, having discovered she was an only child living alone with her Austrian refugee mother, who'd suffered considerably as a result of the war, a sort of common link was forged. I'm pretty sure that taking her home during those dark winter evenings began as a genuine gesture of help. I was someone for her to talk to, someone who cared for her wellbeing and safety. I would comfort her if her mother was upset and particularly if her mother was upset with her. For a bright young teenager to sometimes feel chastised like a child when returning home was difficult. It was impossible for me to comprehend the anguish and fear her mother must have been going through, seeing her only daughter, one of the few stabilising factors in her life, slowly growing away from her. I quickly became a willing support for her, somebody to lean on and share those difficult moments in her life – that somebody also being equally in need of help and companionship.

Inevitably the bond strengthened, particularly as, in the company of her friends and whilst participating in the movement's activities, she shed many of her burdens and tensions; becoming a beautiful, vivacious young woman, enjoying her youth. To see the change in her demeanour each time we approached her home was nearly as harrowing for me as it was devastating for her. Nevertheless, as the youth leader I should have known better and not allowed my own frayed and sensitive emotions to overtake me, something that seems to have occurred at times in my life. Whether this tendency was the result of the loss of parents so early in my life, being forced to leave my foster family, the real lack of consistent family life and family role models, my constantly moving from place to place, of changing cultures when so young, or just part of my character, I don't know.

We were both on different types of rebound, though not in the usual relationship-oriented sense of the word. I was still coming to terms with the loss of a very close family member, my brother, while she was grappling with a mother's love that had turned into an obsessive hold. We were two rather lost souls that gently touched but maybe never really connected. At that particular moment, we seemed to fulfil an emotional need in each other and soon she was expecting our child. In retrospect, I was far too naïve and vulnerable and she was much too young.

For a youth movement that preached a clean and pure, sexless lifestyle before marriage, my situation was unpardonable. We were married in a register office in London and my term as a youth leader came to an abrupt end. My pangs of guilt were overwhelming for having to leave Trudy and the boys without the possibility of my being able to help them any further. Before leaving however, after many meetings and much haranguing, I managed to obtain the princely sum of £100 from the Austrian Restitution Committee as a special financial donation to help Trudy and my nephews. Not much even in those days, but better than nothing.

We would live in Israel – for me returning home and for Yona the fulfilment of the idealistic dream promoted by the movement to emigrate to the Holy Land. We travelled to Israel via Brussels and the World Trade Fair; then onward for an obligatory visit to Vienna, before continuing to Athens for yet another sailing across the Mediterranean. Back home in Merchavya all started well, at least for a short time. I felt comfortable and secure in the knowledge that I was accepted for the person I was. My wife was made welcome, especially by Urge and Eliezer who went out of their way to befriend her but, I think, being pregnant so young, not knowing anyone in the Kibbutz nor speaking the language, life proved very difficult for her.

I was back to teaching English. It was a wonderful stage from which I could demonstrate, at least to my young audience, one of the few areas in which I was relatively proficient. It was an outlet that allowed me to submerge a growing unease with my personal relationship. My wife was experiencing pregnancy during the sweltering hot summer without the help or comfort of family or close friends. I'm sure any blame attributed to me expanded in her mind ten-fold during that period, coupled with the physical and emotional difficulties of her circumstances. Whatever I said, or tried to do, to alleviate her suffering was taken the wrong way and interpreted as a negative action on my part. The consequence was for me to feel ever guiltier, a trait that has, I believe, been part of my character for as long as I can remember. There was however, some light at the end of the tunnel.

Our beautiful daughter Rameet – a derivation of 'high ridge' in Hebrew – was born in October 1958. What a wonderful experience to feel for the first time such a small bundle in your arms and know that you were instrumental in creating and bringing a perfect new human being into this world. No thoughts then of what it would be like twenty years hence, just the immediate natural joy of becoming a father. Maybe, not having any memories of my own parents made it particularly special. For a short time, Rameet's birth relieved the immediate tension. For me, life wasn't bad; after all, I was amongst friends with whom I'd grown up during my adolescence, and I was part of a familiar community. We had a room with facilities, a clothing allocation and meals – admittedly not of the gourmet variety – and Rameet was well looked after during working hours in the children's house. The period after work and before dinner was allocated to quality time with children, with nothing to distract parents from playing with and giving their full and undivided attention to their offspring. There can't be many systems today where that's possible. It was a lifestyle I felt comfortable with. Possession of material goods never constituted a priority for me and that has never changed.

Urge and Eliezer doted on the baby, much like grandparents would. Even Auntie Irene came to visit and later seemed pleased to invite us for the occasional weekend to Haifa to stay with her and Dolphie. Being near Afula it wasn't so far for us to get to Haifa and this proved quite a therapeutic change for both of us; away from the heat, daily routine and squabbling, into the arms of relative luxury. Unfortunately, life appeared to become ever more intolerable for Yona – no immediate family, not knowing the language and, I suspect, a touch of postnatal depression all contributed to her desire to leave Merchavya. Her goal was a move to Kibbutz Zikim, near the Gaza Strip, where many of the members from the youth club in London, who were friends of hers, were living. My feelings of guilt and my wish to try and help her over this difficult period gave me no option but to accede to her wishes.

So, when Rameet was less than a year old we moved to Kibbutz Zikim some distance away. It was near Ashkelon a good two hours from where we were.

Kibbutz Zikim, with daughter Rameet, 1959/1960

Though based on the same principles as Merchavya, the atmosphere on Zikim was very different. For a start, the majority of members on Merchavya were old-timers, most of whom had migrated to what was then Palestine from Central and Eastern Europe before the war. Many came for ideological reasons, several with first class academic qualifications. Merchavya's second generation was already an integral part of Israeli society.

Zikim was a much younger and smaller settlement with members less integrated, the next generation of kibbutzniks still in nappies. To me the relationships between individuals seemed pretty strained and much more personal compared with what I was used to. Everything was less organised and the standard of living was far more basic. Zikim is located on the border of the Gaza Strip, then under Egyptian rule. At the time, the Strip was inhabited by a teeming population of very poor Palestinians. Security was a much bigger issue there; night watch really meant staying awake and alert. On the positive side, the sea was only a few hundred metres away and at night you could hear the waves breaking on the shore. Unfortunately, I hardly knew any of the members and, although I became friendly with several, this was not a happy period in my life.

My wife quickly acclimatised to her surroundings but our relationship didn't improve much. No matter what I did, invariably I was castigated for not being more thoughtful, tactful or caring. And then, much to my surprise, the tension suddenly relaxed. I was soon to find out that whatever I didn't or couldn't provide there was someone else happily doing so behind my back. It all started when she was supposedly on a course outside the kibbutz. The other person, also married and with two children, was attending the same course. When I found out – not from my wife of course – the shock was indescribable. I know we hadn't been married for long, and for much of the time were either at each other hammer and tongs or suffering long, sullen silences, but for me it was my very own first family, one I truly believed would be for life and that would give me the love and stability I was searching for. There was no way back and we agreed to divorce.

It is one thing when a marriage breaks up and one of the partners moves away but quite another in a small isolated community like a kibbutz where the newly established couple make a home literally two or three doors away. The emotional turmoil for me was quite unbearable. All I wanted to do was return to the more familiar surroundings

of Merchavya, my 'home' kibbutz. I'd been living in Zikim
for a couple of years or more but it had not worked out for
me. I asked to take Rameet with me but my ex wouldn't
allow it. I tried to cope with the situation for a while, mainly
because of my daughter whom I loved and with whom I
had great fun crawling on the lawn and playing hide and
seek behind the bushes. But the long, lonely evenings
proved excruciatingly difficult.

I found several jobs outside Zikim one of which was to
work for Mapam, the kibbutz political party, during the
forthcoming elections. I was stationed in Nazareth for
several months and have to admit it was quite an
experience. Mingling with the local Arab population, trying
to persuade them that our left-wing party would look after
their interests more honestly than any other political outfit,
was a totally new experience. If Mapam had got into power
it may have looked at the plight of the Arab population
more favourably than the others. Sadly, none of the political
parties put this issue at the top of their agenda, or made real
efforts to integrate the indigenous Israeli-Arab population
into the newly developing Israeli society. They were always
perceived as the enemy within. Treating them as such
inevitably created just that. As it was, I found counting and
re-counting the votes through the night until the early
hours of the morning rather exciting. The elections didn't
help Mapam much and it remained a small opposition
party in the Knesset, with little influence on the actions of
the charismatic Prime Minister, Ben Gurion.

I was desperately unhappy at Zikim apart from the joy
of being with my daughter who was already four years old.
Out the blue I was approached to return to England, to

Manchester, where a youth leader was needed for a temporary post for a few months. I had done this work for the movement before and I was delighted that there was an opportunity for me to escape Zikim.

It was another change, in an already fairly chaotic life, this time separating me from my young daughter and saw me, once again, on my own, taking a lonely step into unknown territory.

Chapter Ten

Manchester – Israel,   *aged 27 -32*

It is from the midst of this putrid sewer that the greatest river of human industry springs up and carries fertility to the whole world. From this foul drain pure gold flows forth. Here it is that humanity achieves for itself both perfection and brutalization, that civilization produces its wonders, and that civilized man becomes again almost a savage.

Alexis de Tocqueville on Manchester, 1835

I left Israel on an unusually warm winter's day in early January 1963. The sky was solid blue with not a cloud on the horizon. There was an uneasy anticipation of an impending drought, which for the Israeli agricultural settlements spelt gloom and for the public at large a dread of water shortages throughout the long hot summer months.

I arrived in England at the start of what was to become one of the longest and coldest winters on record. In a matter of a few short hours I had been transported, courtesy of an El-Al Boeing 707, from a warm, sunny and somewhat dry landscape to a country covered in freezing ice and snow - a scene that wouldn't change dramatically until early March. Had I had an inkling of such a cold and frosty prospect, I might have tried to delay my departure by a few months, emotional strains notwithstanding.

First, I had to concentrate on finding accommodation, get used to the Mancunian accents and overcome the more troublesome hurdle of making sense of the contradictory directions I was being given. The weather conditions had provided a wonderful excuse to cancel as many public transport routes as possible. When I did finally discover a bus that would take me to my destination, the landscape through which we travelled proved ominously dark and dreary. Long rows of small grey houses stood sandwiched together, not dissimilar to rows of old books precariously held up by flimsy uprights on either side. One could imagine that, like a pack of cards, the slightest movement would send the bricks and mortar holding the fabric together, crumbling into a heap of rubble. Not even the covering of what was once white snow, now a dirty brownish colour, could hide or alleviate the rather depressing realisation slowly penetrating through me that the months ahead were not going to prove a cosy ride.

By the time I reached the Manchester Bayit, situated at the far end of Bury Old Road, I was tired, hungry and very cold. The Bayit did not live up to its name at all. It was dark, damp, freezing and devoid of even the basic essentials like food. Not really what you would expect from a home. I wondered what I'd let myself in for. There wasn't a living soul around except for the next-door neighbour who, after suspiciously eyeing me up and down and exchanging some unfriendly words, reluctantly handed over the keys.

Straight back out into the dark, icy air, and it was only three in the afternoon. There weren't many supermarkets around at that time and probably not too many to be found in the area today. Fortunately, I discovered a small grocery store somewhere along the road and bought some food supplies before making my way back through the freezing fog. By the time I returned my fingers were numb, my feet felt like ice blocks and I was sure my nose was about to drop off. I was desperate for something warm and nourishing. What wouldn't I have given to be back in the warm climate I'd just come from?

A further unwelcome surprise awaited me. At that particular moment, what I hankered for more than anything was a hot drink, but when I turned on the tap to fill the kettle all I got was a few drops of brownish-coloured liquid, and hollow creaking and clanging pipe noises followed by a deathly silence. No water in the kitchen or for that matter anywhere else in the house. It didn't take a stroke of genius to work out that the Bayit's ancient pipes had frozen. There wasn't much I could do so I wrapped up as warm as possible and ventured back out into one of Manchester's famous, murky winter evenings.

Some twenty minutes' fast walking brought me to a small worker's café. It turned out to be a discovery of monumental proportions. There, in a tiny, sparsely furnished, smoke-filled room with tables covered by worn-out, rather grubby, stiff plastic table cloths, I tasted the delights of sizzling hot, greasy bacon, egg and chips, washed down with strong, hot, dark brown, milky tea. It was a gourmet delight, to be savoured for as long as possible. Eating bacon followed by milky tea didn't do me any harm. A case of two minuses equals a plus – or maybe God, for once, taking pity on me and turning a blind eye.

The real lesson I learned that afternoon was how unbelievably friendly the Mancunians are, particularly the down to earth, ordinary folk who are instinctively drawn to strangers in distress. I was quickly informed by the owner and his customers, who were sitting smoking while sipping hot drinks from an assortment of large cracked mugs, that a short bus ride towards town would take me to the local baths where I could fully immerse myself in hot water. For an extra sixpence, they proudly explained, I would even be provided with a clean towel. 'You'll probably have to queue and you're only allowed half an hour,' somebody quickly added. But by that time, I really didn't care. The thought of a hot bath, a change of clothes and the luxury of feeling clean, and more or less being back in the land of living was irresistible.

For a couple of weeks those local baths were a focal point for me and an essential ingredient of living and surviving that cold dark winter in the great city of Manchester. The café became one of my favourite haunts, a wonderfully intimate place where I discovered the intricacies of local politics, how to improve the universe at large and, most importantly, what was happening in the world of sport. Needless to say, anything remotely concerning Manchester United was hotly debated. If they won they could have scored more goals, if they lost, the logic was quite simple – they shouldn't have. And when other topics of conversation began to fizzle out there was always the awful weather to fall back on.

Before leaving Israel, I'd been in contact with my brother Jacques in Australia. On hearing I was going to be based in Manchester for a while he asked me to get in touch with his ex-wife, Jean. I was aware that the divorce had been pretty acrimonious, following which Jean had decided to return to her hometown, Manchester, with their two children, Danny, who now had special needs, and Aviva. Since her return to England there'd been little communication between them.

Be that as it may, I knew Jean pretty well so didn't for a moment consider that getting in touch with her would create a problem. I was keen to see my nephew and niece and discover a few familiar faces. So, one day I rang. The response was quite unexpected.

'I suppose you've come to spy for your brother,' were Jean's first words.

Rather taken aback, I wasn't sure how to respond.

'You know me better than that. I thought it would be rather nice to meet up again and get to know Danny and Aviva,' I eventually replied.

There was a short hesitant silence before she answered.

'OK, let's meet at the Ceylon Tea House in Piccadilly tomorrow afternoon.'

'What about the children?' I asked.

'No, I have to be certain you genuinely want to see them and aren't on some mission for your brother.'

Having just gone through the trauma of separation and divorce myself, I felt sympathetic toward Jean but hadn't bargained for the deep-rooted anger she felt towards Jacques. Anyway, we did meet at the Ceylon Tea House the next day, by which time Jean must have calmed down and got over the shock of my phone call because she proved far more accommodating. She was even amenable to my visiting the children the following weekend which was great.

In the meantime, I'd discovered that there were a few members of the youth movement around, though not many and they were all rather dispersed. I wasn't sure how I was going to persuade Jewish youngsters to come to a club which had little money, possessed few amenities, was in a house devoid of water and with only a couple of small electric-bar heaters to warm the place up, with temperatures never really rising much above freezing until well into the spring. In the circumstances, I'm amazed we managed to conjure up anyone at all. As it was, it took several weeks before enough youngsters had ventured into our cold premises to enable us to organise a semblance of group activities.

As during my previous spell as a youth leader in London, I had to supplement my meagre pay of nineteen shillings a week, again teaching English to foreign students. The remuneration proved even worse and the work less gratifying than when I'd taught in London the last time. This time the majority of my students were Chinese. I couldn't understand them and they hadn't a clue what I was trying to say. However slowly I pronounced the simplest words, their response in English invariably came back sounding Chinese. I never discovered whether their knowledge of the English language improved as a result of my teaching. It was hardly satisfactory for either party but the school didn't seem to care and it was an income, allowing the occasional indulgence of a decent meal. I just continued to do my best. Maybe I should have used the opportunity to learn some Chinese, though I suspect that would have proved way beyond my linguistic abilities.

It may all sound rather awful and gloomy but I do have very fond memories of Manchester. Once the cold, the fog, the mist and the never-ending rain had become part of my daily routine I started getting things into perspective. My main preoccupation and focus, apart from work, became discovering the positive and exciting ingredients that made up the city, and believe it or not there were plenty, even then. The wonderful library for example, where I spent hours sitting in the peace and solitude, in awe of the ability of so many people to remain in virtual silence, heads buried in books for long periods of time. The most inspiring moments were those spent meandering along rows and rows of books of all sizes, whose spines displayed a multitude of subjects to choose from. It was sheer unadulterated joy, a place where you could discover a book on any conceivable topic; from local history and the arts to science fiction at the outer reaches of the universe. The library was somewhere I could lose myself in all the wonderful images produced by all those books, without anyone disturbing me.

I've always loved books and when I found the open-air book market, not far from Manchester Piccadilly Station, a whole new world opened up. Like in the library, there were books of all descriptions: some crumpled, often earmarked, others held together between old decaying covers but, most importantly, all telling different tales; of heroes and villains, facts of the past, mysteries, biographies – you name it. The market was an open door, inviting one to walk in unhindered and become quickly engulfed by a beguiling imagination. Sadly, in my recent travels to Manchester all that remained of the market was a solitary and lonely bookstall selling second-hand volumes in amongst CDs, videos, DVDs and computer games. It didn't stop me buying a book or two though, if only for old time's sake. You can still occasionally see me wandering between the book stalls under the arches of the South Bank in London.

I soon discovered the Halle Orchestra and their extraordinary conductor, Sir John Barbirolli, whose twenty-first season was being celebrated that year. It was at one of his concerts that I was first mesmerised by the young Daniel Barenboim, watching his fingers skate and dance across the keyboard as I listened to a Mozart piano concerto. Manchester was also in proud possession of an Opera House where I not only experienced my first live opera but also had the privilege of hearing Tito Gobbi perform in *La Traviata*.

Numerous pop concerts were drawing crowds to Manchester's music venues but I never went to any as it was against the youth movement's principles to participate in what they saw as decadent culture. How times have changed. Imagine passing up the opportunity to sit in the audience where the top billing is Helen Shapiro in her prime, with the Beatles on the same programme. I do listen to the Beatles today!

An added bonus was, and undoubtedly still is, the magnificent surrounding countryside, which includes the old canals, once the network for commercial transport between Manchester and the rest of the country. A little further afield, to the south, lies the beautiful wind-swept Peak District. In the opposite direction, but still within striking distance, are the glorious Lake District and the Yorkshire Dales, graced not only with natural contemplative beauty but also endowed with that unique English poetic and literary ambience. It's such a glorious area, full of wide-open spaces where one can hide when one's personal woes, and those of the world at large seem to collide; havens where, when life appears to become unbearable and claustrophobic one can admire nature's quiet beauty in solitude.

There was one person I hadn't yet encountered, Diana. She'd been looking after the youth club while the search went on for a youth leader. When we finally met, the scene couldn't have been more comical. Diana was ill with chicken pox or measles or something similar. Anyway, having waited a couple of weeks there seemed little alternative but to arrange our first meeting in her bedroom – with other members present of course. There we were, sitting around her bed, trying not to catch whatever medical condition she had, discussing how to increase the membership of the club and what to do with the young people when they'd been recruited and, most critically, how to get the water system working again.

It was a rather unusual first introduction. Diana, who came from London, was a second-year student at Manchester University studying social administration. Having been a member of the youth movement in London, she'd continued as a leader during her spare time in Manchester. Both her parents were refugees from Europe; her mother was from Vienna and her father from Romania, via Trieste. Naturally, this set up an immediate point of mutual reference. There seemed to be instinctive feelings of interest, certainly on my part, of wishing to learn a little more about the other's character, family background, beliefs and general outlook on life. Even lying unwell in her bed, she exuded the aura of a vivacious, intelligent and very attractive young woman. Whether she was ever going to be attracted to me – a divorcee with a child, and eight years older than her – was an entirely different matter.

We worked well together, and had few major disagreements. There was, at that time, an annual Greater Manchester Youth Drama Festival. We decided to enter the club with an act from an Arnold Wesker play. The rehearsals and organisation for the event took up an inordinate amount of time but proved great fun. Diana, who had an intuitive understanding and love of English language and literature, took over the main role of producer. I never actually worked out why she hadn't studied English; parental pressure to study a vocational subject probably overrode the desire to pursue the subject she really loved. Or maybe the movement persuaded her that social administration was a more useful area of study. I became the general dogsbody — making sure the rehearsals took place, sometimes even overseeing them, finding all the props and equipment that was required and, most importantly, cajoling the actors not just to turn up but to make some effort to be on time.

The great day arrived. We were all there far too early, actors keyed up and nervously tramping up and down behind the stage with scripts in hand, repeating lines with expressive and ever-changing facial contortions. My role, at the advanced age of twenty-eight, had become a sort of calming elder statesman to these worried youngsters who at that particular point in time, probably felt the entire burden of the world on their shoulders. In the event we did pretty well and won third prize amongst the dozen or so entries. It called for a celebration, though not of the alcoholic kind – which the movement frowned on – but afternoon tea and cakes. Those were the days.

While working in Manchester I met various people involved in youth work. The most charismatic was undoubtedly Stan Rowe, a non-Jewish youth and community worker who became club leader of the Jewish Lads Brigade in Manchester. I frequently met him, mainly at the JLB but also a few times in his home where, together with his wife Wendy, we'd have lively discussions, mainly about the wayward direction in which young people were heading, an issue that hasn't altered much fifty years later. Our chats invariably ended in reflecting on the general woes of the world and in particular those of Israel, which also sadly haven't improved greatly.

Stan was an extraordinary man with a wife of a very similar standing who totally shared his ideals. Both were dedicated to youth work, and to promoting inter-faith cooperation and understanding. I expect being the club leader of the Jewish Lads Brigade required an extremely sound understanding of Jewish laws and traditions. Otherwise, who knows what deep waters he could have found himself in? I did keep in touch with Stan for a while after I left Manchester though sadly he died in 1992, while still only in his sixties.

There were, of course, other Jewish clubs. One of these, Habonim, is still around today. It was not as left-wing as our club, Hashomer. Although our clubs didn't have much to do with one another, I knew Habonim's club leader. One day we happened to meet not far from his house. I noticed that his nose was covered by a large bandage.

'What happened?' I asked. "

'Well,' he started, rather sheepishly. 'Yesterday was my son's brit [circumcision]. Unfortunately, I fainted.'

I couldn't help laughing but quickly commiserated. I wonder if he ever told his son.

Around Easter, Diana went to Vienna with her mother to visit a cousin still living there. I think his name was Heinrich. I found out later that his story was yet another chapter in the book of survival against the odds. Quite why he remained in Vienna I don't know. Probably because, like my grandparents and so many other Jews, despite the obvious anti-Semitism that was rife throughout Austria, they never believed things could get as bad as they did. Anyway, he was an avid stamp collector and managed to find refuge with a local family outside the Austrian capital by slowly selling off his treasured collection. When that ran out he was betrayed and spent the last year of the war in concentration camps, but survived.

During Diana's trip, while I was in London spending time with Trudy and my nephews, I received a postcard from Vienna. Diana told me she was having a great time but was looking forward to getting back and meeting up before her term restarted. I vividly remember reading and re-reading the card several times as I walked aimlessly along the streets around Finchley Road Station and wondering what might happen next. I'd so recently come through the fog of a failed marriage. I wondered if Diana was just being friendly or if there was more. I let my thoughts meander: we got on well, had similar aspirations, she was intelligent, attractive and vivacious and we had similar family backgrounds - what could possibly go wrong? Emotions quickly superseded intellectual analysis. Not, I must hasten to add, that I had any doubts in terms of wanting to become involved. I suppose it was more a matter of trying to consider things logically before becoming totally and utterly submerged, which is what happened the moment we met on her return from Vienna. It wasn't a mistake – we were married for nearly twenty years and had two wonderful children.

One of our first outings together took place during the Whitsun holiday at the end of May. We decided to hitchhike through Scotland. My most vivid memory of this particular adventure is the persistent rain that seemed to follow us all the way up to Aberdeen, along the river Dee and as far as our aborted attempt to cross over to the Isle of Skye. Despite the damp, wet, atmosphere that accompanied us we had great fun. For a start, the anticipation involved in wondering whether a vehicle would stop or not, and whether we'd get to our next port of call before dark and find a bed and breakfast before they all closed for the night, was more of an excitement than a bore. Then there was the day a travelling salesman decided to show us around the Highlands to the source of the River Dee, proudly pointing out Balmoral and its glorious grounds from a special vantage point en route. Driving alongside the Dee, he went into ecstasies describing the production of whisky. He obviously didn't feel like working because instead of dropping us in the pouring rain miles from anywhere he took pity and brought us back to

Aberdeen. He certainly conveyed the pride the Scots feel about their whisky, and their country's beautiful landscape, during the time we spent with him. Even the Queen and her Scottish lodgings were admired.

With only two days left we made a futile attempt to visit the Isle of Skye. The rain was so incessant and dense that even if a car had come our way we wouldn't have noticed it until it had passed. Standing forlornly by the side of the road, with water streaming off us, I looked around and tried to focus on the natural beauty we were surrounded by. I realised there was an abundance of rhododendrons on both sides of the road. At the height of the flowering season, they included every conceivable shade of red. Though burdened by the heavy water as they were, we didn't really see them in their full glory; their petals waiting in vain for a glimpse of the sun to reappear in the Scottish skies. Eventually we gave up, crossed over the road and started our homeward journey, glimpsing specks of blue sky somewhere above the Yorkshire Dales.

It was time to meet Diana's parents who knew little about me. I don't think that what they discovered met with their immediate approval, certainly not as far as her mother was concerned. Divorced, father of a young daughter and living on a kibbutz. What kind of a future for her daughter was that? I became very friendly with her father – though who wouldn't? I've rarely come across a nicer, kinder, more intelligent human being. He spoke several languages fluently and always kept up to date with current political issues, in particular those concerning Israel. He was a typical intellectual who, in order to make a living, had set up a small workshop making lamp shades which provided a modest living but probably not the intellectual stimulus his ability deserved.

We got married in a synagogue in Manchester as we were both still based there. Shortly after we were expecting our first child and decided to be in London, near to Diana's family, for the birth. I was looking for some work to tide us over and through a contact from the kibbutz was put in touch with Emmanuel Beirer, an eminent Harley Street gynaecologist. Emmanuel came from Vienna where, in his youth, he'd been a member of the Hashomer Hatzair movement. For a while he'd lived in Kibbutz Beth Alpha, not far from Merchavya. On returning to London he'd set up a private clinic in The Avenue, on the fringes of Regents Park. He was also the founder of a charitable trust, raising funds for his beloved kibbutz. We became friendly and I worked for him on a part-time basis, assisting with the administration of his trust, which helped keep me afloat financially.

Emmanuel was the consultant gynaecologist at the Bethnal Green Hospital so that was where my son Allon was born in 1964, in earshot of the Bow Bells, making him a true cockney. Emmanuel agreed that I could be present at his birth, not such a common occurrence at the time and much to the chagrin of Diana's mother. Such shenanigans would have been unheard of in Vienna. Allon was in no hurry to enter the wide-open space of our universe, so consequently required the gentle persuasion of a pair of forceps, at which point, sadly, I was asked to leave the room. I wasn't actually there when he was born but they managed pretty well, even without my expertise.

Soon after his birth we moved back to Manchester for Diana to finish her degree. I was probably what would be described today as a house husband and looked after Allon while she was studying. Once she had finished we both knew we would be heading to Israel and after going back to London to say farewell to family and friends we set off for Kibbutz Zikim. I had been very unhappy there when I left but was OK about going back as I had Diana with me, my son, and the prospect of seeing my daughter whom I had missed so much. Diana knew many people from London who had gone to live there so was happy with the arrangement too.

While I am sure Diana wanted to make it work, she, like many, found the system on most left-wing kibbutzim that, virtually from birth, babies were cared for and slept in special children's accommodation, rather than at home, very hard to accept. While Diana was aware of this way of life, a topic often discussed and hotly debated during her time in the movement back in the UK, academic theory can be one thing and actual reality quite another.

Sadly, we didn't last long in Zikim which, when I look back, fills me with a sense of some regret. In the main, and even bearing in mind some of its imperfections, kibbutz life provided an environment in which I was happy and felt a sense of basic equality between myself and my fellow human beings. The biggest problem involved in leaving the kibbutz system back then was that not only did you depart virtually empty-handed, you were also made to feel guilty and a traitor for taking such a step and deserting. And yet again I was leaving Rameet.

I was thirty years old and had nothing to show for all the years spent working on the kibbutz; no money and no profession. Our first move was to the nearby port town of Ashdod, primarily to make it easier for me to visit Rameet. Luckily, with the help of Diana's cousin, I found a job as a computer operator at one of the banks in Tel Aviv. This involved frequent night shifts. I can't count the number of times I fell asleep on the bus, missing my stop and having to trek home in the early hours of the morning.

The population of Ashdod was mainly made up of immigrants from North Africa; their culture was very different from the one we'd been brought up in. Our neighbours, for example, very quickly seemed to know more about us than we did about ourselves. For some I suppose it was a diversion from the normal stresses and strains of their own family lives, and their way of being friendly. For Diana, coming from a suburban London upbringing, the culture was pretty alien. To tell the truth, it also irked me. It all came to a head one day as we were waiting our turn at the local surgery. At the best of times, queuing is far from being the favourite Israeli pastime, particularly for those originating from other parts of the Middle East. Anyway, while we were standing there a youngster came up to Diana and, for reasons best known to him, idly hit her with a stick. It wasn't hard, but hard enough for me to take the offending implement break it and throw away the pieces. Within a few minutes I was confronted by several strapping young men, cursing me in Arabic and Hebrew before expressing what a pity it was that Hitler hadn't finished the job. The shock of this statement shook me. Even in anger, how was it possible for a Jew to utter such words to someone who'd had to live with the results of the Holocaust? Talk about diverse cultures, backgrounds and upbringings – and all sharing the same religion.

After that little episode Ashdod had no chance of keeping us. We moved to the more 'civilised', middle class, western area of Kiryat Ono, an outer suburb of Tel Aviv, where most of the inhabitants were either second generation, or had come from Europe. Diana was pregnant again and I had just managed to find a new higher paid job as computer room manager at a different bank. It was time for a holiday and a visit to Diana's parents before the imminent job change took place. No sooner had we arrived in London than the 1967 war broke out and I found myself again on the brink of another major upheaval.

I can well recall making my way to Heathrow each day to try to get a flight home, without success, until the third attempt. Each time I returned to Diana's parents the TV was showing Topol, the leading actor in the recently released *Fiddler on the Roof*, making the same abortive attempts. When eventually I managed to get back to Israel I quickly realised I was too late and that my services were not required. The Six Day War was virtually over but a new set of problems was about to commence.

Diana had remained in London with her parents and Allon. Being pregnant and with family pressure no doubt swaying the day, it soon became clear that she wasn't keen to return to Israel. For me it was another of those stumbling hurdles of life that I have constantly been confronted with. Always, it seems, just around the corner to test my strength, or weakness, of character. What was I to do? Lose my family or leave my life in Israel. I couldn't face the former so there was no choice. I had limited work experience as a computer operator; I had to give up a new and better-paid job; I had no money to speak of and ten post-dated cheques, made out for the apartment we were renting in Kiryat Ono, to be redeemed. I had the daunting prospect of being jobless in London and top of the list I would again be so far away from Rameet.

I was pretty busy for a few weeks sorting out the mess. It was only once everything was more or less under control that it dawned on me that I was about to leave the country that had been my home for eighteen years, a longer period than either of my previous two sojourns and again, as in both of those cases, it wasn't a step I'd planned, or would have taken if left to my own devices. The idea of travelling to an uncertain future with a pregnant wife, a young son, no home, hardly any money, no real profession and having to leave my daughter behind was indeed a daunting and very sad prospect.

Chapter Eleven

London Wembley Park, aged 32 - 42

I am the family face;
Flesh perishes, I live on
Projecting trait and trace
Through time to times anon
And leaping from place to place
Over oblivion.

Thomas Hardy

It had been an integral part of my youth and young adulthood, so walking away from kibbutz life was a difficult internal struggle. The kibbutz had, after all, become my home and was an environment in which I felt comfortable and relatively settled. Now, the idea of turning my back on the country where I'd lived for the longest period in my life, and for which I'd fought a war, was quite depressing. Even more disturbing was the knowledge that I had to start all over again, close another chapter of my life and leave behind numerous friends and relatives. Compounding this sadness was the burden of my having to part from Rameet, my firstborn. At the time there seemed little alternative if I didn't want to be dragged through the emotional turmoil of another failed marriage. I suspect, deep down inside I felt a hidden fear of my life becoming a canvas blazoned with people I'd been close to who'd disappeared into the horizon.

As I emerged from customs at Heathrow I suddenly found myself confronted by a little boy who, after eyeing me up and down suspiciously for several moments, suddenly made a wild dash into my arms. My mood changed dramatically. All the misgivings I'd been mulling over during the flight somehow evaporated, at least for the time being. 'About the same age as I was when separated from my parents,' I mused, embracing my small son tightly. Then, gazing into his warm, vulnerable, admiring eyes I could only conceive of a bright and positive family future. I saw no point in dwelling on the past.

Diana had somehow managed to rent a small bungalow in Wembley Park, not far from the stadium. It was up to me to find work if we were going to pay the rent and have food on the table. I'd written a couple of short computer programs while working for the bank in Israel but decided to skip a rung and elevate myself to the role of systems analyst. My challenge was to create a CV which would make my computing experience look more impressive than it actually was, without straying too far from the truth.

Several weeks of intensive letter-writing and phoning around landed me a position. It was my army career, and participation in the 1956 Suez campaign as an Israeli officer, that had come to my rescue. This part of my CV appealed to Leslie Fellner, the owner of a small recruitment consultancy firm, who finally found me work. Leslie was a real gentleman; of South African-Jewish origin. He was far more impressed by my army background than any possible technical computing ability I might have possessed. It took a few ghastly mistakes before I managed to work out the fundamentals of computer systems analysis but luckily, I'm a reasonably fast learner, otherwise even my military escapades wouldn't have saved me.

The office of the company I worked for was located just off the Strand, which gave me an unexpected opportunity to discover London. I thoroughly enjoyed wandering along the Strand into Trafalgar Square, down the Mall or toward the Houses of Parliament and the Embankment during lunch breaks. There was always the option to stride in the other direction and find myself in Covent Garden, then still a proper market. Or to cross the Thames over Waterloo Bridge to one of my favourite buildings in London, the Royal Festival Hall. Stopping in the middle of this wonderful bridge, I would often gaze at those great historic edifices, so unique to London: St Paul's Cathedral and the Old Bailey on one side, the Houses of Parliament and Big Ben on the other.

As I stood staring down at the river below I tried to cast my mind back some twenty-eight years to when I'd first arrived on the *Warsawa*, along the same stretch of water. I hit a total blank, nothing. No memories came flooding back then or at any time before or since. No matter how frequently I stand there contemplating, watching the crammed tourist boats disappearing beneath the bridge or viewing the new buildings forever rising on the banks of the Thames, nothing, it seems, will ever bring back memories of the earliest part of my life.

I suspect that my affection for London, and in particular the area around the Embankment, had its roots in these strolls. Forty years later I still derive enormous pleasure from strolling along the banks of the Thames, now with the added bonus of the National Theatre, the London Eye, the Tate Modern, the Globe and several new bridges spanning the river. Can there be anything more exciting than scouring through the hundreds of second-hand books heaped on wooden trestle tables outside the National Film Theatre - the icing on the cake discovering a book I'd been looking for underneath a pile of dusty, shabby-looking paperbacks.

It had been wonderful of Leslie to get me a job but I soon realised that I needed to move on, and look to earn more money, so I started to seek alternative employment. I eventually found it with the Thomson Organisation, then owners of Times Newspapers. My main recollection of the time spent there is of constant wrangling with the unions. It fell on me to explore the possibility of computerising the cumbersome typesetting process then in place. At one point, it was planned that I should conduct a study of the work being carried out in the compositor's room. I'd barely opened the door when a stocky young man walked up and, in no uncertain terms, demanded to know who'd given me permission to enter the holy sanctuary. My explanation and assurance that my visit had been agreed well in advance with the 'father of the chapel' (the union leader) held no water. 'I'm the deputy father of the chapel and nobody told me you were coming,' he announced. 'So, if you don't leave immediately we're going on strike.'

As compensation, I was sent to Germany to discover how the well-organised Germans were able to convert their newspaper production from being extremely labour-intensive into something more modern, pared down and electronic. At a printing house located in the small town of Württemberg, near Stuttgart, I discovered that, despite their fame for methodical and technical advance, the German printing system seemed even more cumbersome than the one I was supposed to be helping to bring up to date. It seems strange, but if anything, the fact is they were over-organised. Each member of staff had his or her specific allocated task which couldn't overlap with anything anybody else was responsible for. It became quite apparent that most of the employees had little knowledge of what any of their colleagues' work involved. Consequently, if anything went wrong in one area, the entire system collapsed until a specialist, suitably attired in a white overall, could be found to remedy the breakdown.

I was booked into a Stuttgart hotel, in the middle of the red-light district. Places to eat were difficult to find and when I did they were dimly lit and meekly hidden behind the glaring lights promoting the pleasures of the flesh. I didn't really learn much from that trip, except that so many of us appear to be under the illusion that the grass must be greener on the other side.

My second daughter, Liora, was born just before I joined the Thomson Organisation. Mr Beirer looked after Diana again, this time at his private clinic on The Avenue. I was present at Liora's birth; no need to be chucked out this time, my second daughter was in much more of a hurry to enter the world than her brother. However, I managed to make the mistake of announcing that we had another boy. It was the initial sight of a shock of dark hair that fooled me. No Bow Bells for my daughter, instead the comfortable and genteel surroundings of a private clinic in St John's Wood, within sight of Regents Park, which I am sure suited her much better.

It was obvious that any move toward the technical modernisation of typesetting in the British newspaper industry was going to be slow and laborious. I well remember the day I happened to be in the lift alone with Lord Thomson. On discovering the work I was involved with he commented, 'I don't know how we will ever move forward - strikes threatened every other day, obstacles put up against any ideas for modernisation. To top it all,' he continued, 'just imagine, last week I found myself sitting next to one of our senior union officials in a first-class seat to Toronto, travelling to an international union conference. No doubt to find new ridiculous reasons for calling strike actions. On my expense, of course,' he quickly added.

Luckily, just as he'd finished his tirade, the lift doors opened, so no response was required. It was the only contact I ever had with him.

Not long before I had joined them, the Thomson Organisation had taken over a number of holiday companies, including Britannia Airways. They'd begun to set about changing the face of the package holiday industry. Some extraordinarily forward-looking concepts, coupled with the astute marketing of cheap winter breaks to Majorca, suddenly led to a huge surge in demand. I was hastily moved to Thomson Holidays' office in Greater London House - the old Black Cat Cigarette building, opposite Mornington Crescent underground station. My task was to sort out the enormous piles of paper that had accumulated as a result of the boom in trade.

I tend to believe that our control over destiny is limited, and frequently subject to vagaries that are disconnected to anything we might have planned. Our personal initiatives don't necessarily take us in the direction initially foreseen. The more I look back and contemplate the past, the more I begin to see how many imponderables there are in this maze of life. If my own history up until then had seemed to encapsulate these constant variables and unforeseen situations, the new world of the travel industry would prove to be sprinkled with similar phenomena of the unexpected.

On arriving at Greater London House, I was immediately confronted by a room full of boxes, all overflowing with booking forms. Nobody seemed able to explain why they were there or when they'd arrived. When I finally tracked down the person responsible he was sitting comfortably in his office reading a magazine. He told me that he'd been waiting to see how long it would take his staff to do something about the problem. It seemed a rather bizarre approach to the situation and didn't take long for me to grasp that I'd been given a pretty thorny task. Frantic calls from members of the public were already coming in, demanding to know why they hadn't had a response to completed booking forms and deposits sent in several weeks earlier.

Drastic action was called for. I was given permission to take over the dining room and bring in temporary staff to try and sort the mess out. It took about a dozen of us working solidly for around six weeks to bring matters under control. At the same time, plenty of reorganisation was going on within the company at the end of which I found myself suddenly and very unexpectedly elevated to the position of Client Services Director. This included looking after the booking administration, client complaints – which were rapidly accumulating – and scheduled flight negotiations. I've never quite worked out how I went from being a lowly computer operator in 1967 to becoming a director of one of the UK's largest travel companies three years later. Talk about being in the right place at the right time.

Several incidents spring to mind as I reflect on my ten years at Thomson's, many that highlighted the delicate balance between success and failure, life and death. I vividly recall driving to Dorking with Allon and Liora to visit my foster mother one Sunday – one of the unexpected bonuses of being back in the UK was that I could resume visiting her. The radio was on and somewhere near Chessington Zoo there was a sudden break in the programme for a special announcement: 'A Turkish aeroplane flying from Istanbul to London has just crashed near Paris. As yet, there is no news of any survivors.'

Initially, the announcement didn't really sink in. Then, several moments later, I suddenly realised that there'd been about forty Thomson passengers on the plane. I quickly turned around and made my way back to London and the office. The atmosphere when we arrived was grim. Somehow, and quite illogically, we felt a huge sense of responsibility for the crash. Forty clients, from all corners of the UK had booked a weekend holiday, never to return. Inevitably there were many heart-breaking stories. The one that has always stuck in my mind involved a young man whose wife had been on the plane in the company of another man, without the husband's knowledge. He was, understandably, distraught and at one point even threatened to sue us. It takes considerable time and effort to overcome such a tragedy, totally unforeseen and unexpected, that devastated the lives of the close families and friends of the deceased holidaymakers. In the case of the young man, the knowledge that his wife had died while betraying him must have haunted him ever since.

After the huge success of cheap winter sun holidays came the launch of city weekend breaks, the most memorable being a weekend in Moscow for the princely sum of £49. This offer resulted in a visit from the Soviet ambassador and it fell on me to look after him. At one point, one of the sales girls asked if there were nationals from other countries who wouldn't be given a visa to enter the Soviet Union. 'Only two,' the ambassador replied, 'South Africa and Israel.' Returning to my office for a coffee, the Ambassador enquired, 'Have you been to Moscow, Mr Reich?'

'No,' I said.

'Why ever not?' he asked.

'Unfortunately, I have one of those passports you refuse to give a visa to,' I explained.

'Which one is that?'

'Israeli,' I retorted.

'Don't worry, Mr Reich, I will arrange special dispensation for you,' he assured me.

He was true to his word. A few months later – by which time I'd become a British citizen anyway – I travelled to the Soviet capital as the guest of Intourist.

I made my second visit to the Soviet Union several years later, while working for Thomas Cook. That trip didn't go without incident. We'd decided to set up a summer holiday programme using the beaches of Sochi on the Black Sea. As I was a director of Thomas Cook, Intourist once again invited me as their guest. The standard of the resort was probably just about acceptable but the exceptionally low prices, and the idea of holidays behind the Iron Curtain, more than made up for the huge nondescript buildings and lack of facilities. We'd more or less decided that on returning to the UK I'd sign an agreement but, not for the first time, political events intervened. I was waiting for a much-delayed connection to Moscow when my Russian guide informed me that the Soviet army had just invaded Afghanistan. We were watching the black and white television monitor in the waiting room showing huge crowds demonstrating in Trafalgar Square.

'What's that all about?' I asked the guide.

'These are our British colleagues marching in support of the Soviet invasion,' he replied.

'Really,' I said. 'Actually, that looks like footage of the anti-nuclear demonstrations and walk to Aldermaston that happened some time ago,' I informed my host.

Such are the ways of public brain-washing. There was, of course, no way that the local population would have any idea that what they were seeing was anything different from the explanation given them by the authorities, through the television commentator.

I've just gone a little ahead of myself – Moscow was not the only city break Thomson promoted. Amongst the many cities on offer was Jerusalem, a destination I persuaded the marketing department to include. As a consequence, one day I found myself in a meeting with the management of El Al's London office. The idea was to block-book some seventy seats on a weekly basis throughout the winter months. El Al's main concern was that their ethnic 'seat only' traffic would be diluted and that we would not strictly adhere to an agreement of only selling full packages. Comments like 'Don't believe a word he says,' started passing between them in Hebrew. They would have had no idea that they were likely to be sitting opposite a Hebrew-speaker. I waited a few minutes and then in my best Hebrew interjected. Totally taken aback, and struck silent by my fluency in their language, we resumed negotiations successfully.

My time at Thomson's spanned the demise of Clarksons Travel as well as the takeover of Harry Goodman's Intersun and Lunn Poly. It didn't take long to discover Harry's unique selling methods – heavily overbook all the popular, high season destinations and then, when it's too late for potential clients to find an alternative, offer the unsold packages to people desperate for a continental holiday. This system was bound to flounder sooner or later. Sorting out the resulting mess, with irate clients angrily telling my staff, in no uncertain terms, what they thought of the situation, was pretty stressful for those having to respond.

I even had a brush with the intelligence service. Out of the blue, I received a phone call from a gentleman proclaiming that he was from the Foreign Office and would I be prepared to meet him as he wanted to ask me a few questions concerning my dealings with Soviet Aeroflot airline staff. His proposal included lunch at Wheelers in

Piccadilly. A free lunch, why not? It couldn't possibly do any harm.

While the meal was very good the questions were somewhat bizarre.

'Did you realise the airline's manager wasn't really an aviator but actually a member of the KGB?'

'No,' I replied. 'It had never occurred to me.'

'Well, I can assure you that is the case,' I was informed. 'So, you'll understand why we need as much information about him as possible. Do you meet in his office?'

'Yes.'

'Where does he sit?'

'Behind his desk.'

'Does he ask you any questions unrelated to your work?'

'No!'

And so it went on for about an hour. Unfortunately, my so-called intelligence didn't prove very helpful. There were no further invitations to lunch.

During this period Rameet's mother had returned to the UK with her family but had left Rameet, now about twelve years old, in Israel with her 'kibbutz parents'. Inevitably, this resulted in much soul-searching on my part until with the help of my aunt I decided to bring her to London to stay with us. It had been my instinctive reaction to this unexpected situation and not one in which I necessarily stopped to consider all the likely consequences, even if I could have. At times, the predicament one is confronted with, and the consequential actions embarked upon in good faith, take on a life of their own, as they did in this case.

The atmosphere at home became difficult. Looking back, it shouldn't really have come as much of a surprise. After all, we were living in a small two-bedroom bungalow with two young children. At the same time, having experienced the disappearance of both her parents at different but vulnerable ages, Rameet understandably needed and demanded attention. For a while Rameet went to live with her mother but it didn't work out. The solution, not wholly satisfactory, was a boarding school just to the west of London, from where Rameet could at least spend her holidays with us. During this time, I managed to visit her every few weeks, although the instability inevitably affected her relationship with us. I have frequently cast my mind back to that period and pondered whether I could, or should have found a better solution. Even now, so many years later, I'm still none the wiser. The only course was to continue communication and hope that, gradually, relationships would be repaired on the basis of mutual trust, shared understanding and respect. Rameet has grown up to be a wonderful caring person both in her professional and her family life. I am proud of her and what she has achieved and enjoy the times we share together with her husband and children.

A few years later Allon had reached his thirteenth birthday and according to Jewish custom had his bar mitzvah, at which he performed quite outstandingly. 'A musical voice and beautifully recited,' the rabbi noted after the ceremony. Well, what else would one expect from the grandson of a stand-in *chazan* (cantor) for the High Holidays in Vienna? It was one of those few occasions when most of my close relatives from all corners of the globe somehow managed to gather to celebrate a special family event. Auntie Irene came from Israel, and my brother Jacques, his wife Susan and family flew over from Australia. The sight of the sixty or so guests milling around in the garden, all there to celebrate my eldest son's bar mitzvah, and his first foray into young adulthood, gave me a great sense of pride and belonging. Looking back, it was a wonderful experience for all of us, family and guests.

Allon had also managed to gain entry to one of the few remaining grammar schools in north London, William Ellis. This was the spur we needed to move from Wembley and the madding crowds from the Wembley Stadium. With us went some lasting memories of England vs. Scotland games. These fixtures tended to be followed by kilted Scots peeing over our front garden wall after invariably losing the match.

Chapter Twelve

London Muswell Hill, aged 43-52

There are no conditions of life to which a man cannot get accustomed, especially if he sees them accepted by everyone around him.

Leo Tolstoy, *Anna Karenina*

Muswell Hill, with its Edwardian homes and Alexandra Palace perched at its peak, lording over glorious vistas and vast stretches of London, was an entirely different proposition to Wembley Park. The house we moved into was a typical example, with its beautiful Art Nouveau stained glass divider in the entrance hall. I think that was probably the deciding factor when we chose it as our home. After all, with an annual salary of £9,000, the asking price of £29,000 was somewhat beyond our means.

The main reason was to be closer to Allon's new school but once we'd made the move it felt like a breath of fresh air to have escaped the somewhat claustrophobic atmosphere of Northwest London. What could possibly befall us in the rarefied atmosphere of nearby Highgate with its famous cemetery, in the midst of which stands the rather vulgar grave of Karl Marx; or to find ourselves virtual neighbours of Hampstead, home to the aspiring elite and in walking distance of elegant Kenwood House in the heart of its wonderful Heath?

Not only had we landed in a lovely part of London surrounded by woods and parks but we had also succeeded in moving into larger, more desirable accommodation, and we were nearer to old friends, people we had known from the movement all those years earlier and from the kibbutz in Israel. We were just a short bus ride from Allon's school and Liora had started at the local primary, five minutes' walk from home. Once settled, we became increasingly re-involved with the people we'd known from the past but under different circumstances and in a new environment. Living together in Israel on a kibbutz is not the same as being neighbours of up and coming middle class residents of Muswell Hill.

Instead of the regular commotion of seething, voluble football crowds that we'd known in Wembley, we could now enjoy exhibitions at Alexandra Palace, as well as the bi-annual Antique Fairs, to which we became regular visitors, mainly as buyers, though on occasion also as sellers. The serene waters of the small boating pond behind the Palace, it's fascinating history and the views from the top of the hill were all significant added bonuses.

Meanwhile, at work the Jerusalem itineraries were proving a great success and, as a result, my name came to the attention of several Jewish tour operators. One of these, Peltours, decided to approach me. I probably shouldn't have succumbed to their overtures but I suppose the idea of becoming a big fish in a small pond was just too appealing. Their managing director at the time told me he was on the verge of retiring and thought I'd be an excellent replacement. After considerable thought, I decided to leave my post as operations director at Thomson Holidays after ten happy years and accepted the offer of managing director of Peltours, only to discover very quickly that I had been misled. Within days of my arrival he told me that he was taking a six-week vacation and promptly left, leaving me holding the baby without any preparation. On returning, refreshed – surprise, surprise – he'd changed his mind about retirement. I've never been very good at accepting hidden agendas so within less than a year I decided to find alternative employment. As it happened, my ex-boss at Thomson's had meanwhile moved to Thomas Cook and was looking for somebody to help him.

And so, I found myself working for Thomas Cook which unfortunately involved commuting from London to Peterborough every day. It was quite a schlep, and a long day to boot. Thomas Cook may have moved into a new and modern building but their working methods were in dire need of an update. The comparison between Thomson and Thomas Cook was stark. While a few of their senior staff were young and forward-looking, the vast majority had spent virtually their entire working lives with the company. Changing their habits was an unenviable task. An almost Dickensian aura permeated the whole office, with clerks bent over paper, all minding their own business and working to their contract hours – at exactly 17.30 everybody got up and left the building, homeward bound. Some of the old timers could even remember a time when permission had to be sought from one's immediate supervisor to get married.

Staff seemed quite oblivious to the fact that a number of the company's projects were losing money. There was one that stood out in particular. Every ten years the inhabitants of the German village of Oberammergau put on a festival during the summer months that revolved around the performance of a passion play. Celebrating the miracle that the Black Death raging through Europe had somehow left their village unscathed, the festival is a thanksgiving to God for stopping the dreaded plague from entering Oberammergau. The fact that it was an isolated community far from any major city seems to have been overlooked. Anyway, Thomas Cook had virtually sole monopoly on selling some twenty thousand packages for this very popular event but, despite having several years to prepare, the company still managed to lose money. My arrival at the end of 1979, in readiness for the 1980 festival, was far too late to have much effect except to help reduce the losses.

The claustrophobic atmosphere at Thomas Cook was a stark contrast to the atmosphere of the kibbutz, and to my working experience in a young and forward-looking company like Thomson Holidays. Directors' board lunches, for example, didn't appeal to me so I rarely went. On one of my infrequent visits the other directors turned around, as I entered, and asked why I had come.

'What's the problem?' I asked.

'It's Yom Kippur,' was the prompt reply. So much for my religious observance!

I spent nine years with the company; most of the time trying to remind all who would listen that their founder was an innovator, constantly in search of new ideas and ways of offering adventures in leisure travel. A member of the Temperance Society living in Market Harborough in the middle of the industrial revolution, Thomas Cook became concerned that factory workers were spending most of their hard-earned money on drink. To lure the men away from the delights of alcohol he came up with the idea of organising outings for workers' families. His first venture was to charter a train. The railway had just begun to expand and was fast becoming the travel vogue. At the same time he negotiated with one William Paget Esq. for his party's use of Paget's Park in Loughborough when it arrived at the end of the eleven-mile train journey. The price of the excursion included tea and sandwiches and the return journey to Leicester, all for the princely sum of one shilling. Alcohol was banned. It turned out to be a great success, with over five hundred people taking part in this novel adventure. The trip caused huge local excitement, with some three thousand people turning out to see the day trippers off. Most of the bridges along the route were thronged with crowds shouting and waving flags, a sight to behold on a sunny July afternoon in 1841.

It was the beginning of modern day tourism. Before long Cook was organising seaside holidays; including to Liverpool, of all places. A little later he started organising itineraries abroad – initially in Europe – then specialist trips to experience the wonders of the Holy Land and Egypt. Cook's Tours became so well known that they regularly featured in late nineteenth century literature. In one of his advertisements he proudly proclaimed a new and higher standard of service – iron bedsteads in the tents. Unfortunately, Cook's original travel concepts, and innovative and adventurous ideas seemed to have got lost when the company became a national institution. Maybe those who ran Cook's Tours, once it had become established, were more interested in basking in past glories than coming up with new and fresh ideas, in order to keep pace with a rapidly changing world.

Thomas Cook survived nationalisation during the war, became part of British Rail and then was taken over by the Midland Bank, but the company seemed a far cry from its original roots of catering to the intrepid British traveller, taking them to unknown and exciting new destinations.

Having suffered the rigours and pitfalls of Oberammergau, including a couple of nights with the TV production team for Judith Chalmers' programme *Wish You Were Here*, I started looking around for something that could promote the company's original essence. It didn't take long. A couple of visits to the archives yielded some interesting information. In 1884, Thomas Cook the younger was asked by Gladstone to lend help in the planned rescue of General Gordon from Khartoum. History tells us that like so many similar, poorly executed grand ventures, this one also failed. Despite Cook receiving the princely sum of £300,000 for the use of his tourist boats on the Nile, Gordon wasn't saved. This was probably due to the usual dilly-dallying, and umpteen contradictory instructions relayed, and then misdirected, along the way. Not dissimilar to other military disasters during that century and the following one.

I discovered this particular historical gem in 1983, giving me time to try and persuade the powers that be what a wonderful opportunity a centenary trip would be to promote the name of Thomas Cook. To my surprise the idea caught on. In preparation, it involved numerous visits to Egypt, and constant contact with prospective lecturers from the British Museum and history departments at various universities. Somewhere along the line, Central Television decided that the project would make an interesting television documentary. The result was Max Hastings joining us. Filling the boat proved the easy bit – organising an interesting two weeks was a far greater challenge. In the event, every day involved visits to some of the most wonderful archaeological sights the world has to offer, supplemented, for those who were interested, with lectures in the evenings.

1984 turned out to be quite a year for me. Not even Orwell could have predicted.

Having always loved running I had been watching with excitement the growth of the London Marathon from the first one in 1981and decided at the start of 1984 to run. As usual this led me into all kinds of unforeseen directions. For a start, my old friend Maish persuaded me to run for his charity 'Kith and Kids'. Then I came up with the bright idea of asking my sponsors to double the stakes if I ran under four hours which they agreed to. I had really set myself a serious challenge and tried, in the time I had, to train hard. On the April day, I loved the whole experience. I found it very difficult and even walked a bit in the middle but I really felt I had achieved something. I wasn't aware that my son Allon was waiting at the finishing point at Westminster Bridge and at about three hours and fifty-five minutes said to his friends, "Where the bloody hell is he?" Amazingly I finished in three hours and fifty-eight minutes, allowing me to raise some £4,000.

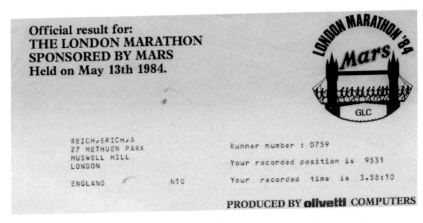

My Marathon result 1984

Unfortunately, I decided to have a hot bath on returning home as a result of which I fainted on to the radiator and found myself needing several stitches at the local Whittington Hospital.

It was my first charity challenge!

I believe my family were proud of my marathon run. But heartache was around the corner as not long after, with twenty years of marriage behind us and two children, Diana told me she was leaving me for someone else. It was the second time in my life that my marriage had failed and my spouse had found someone else to share her life with. It was a huge shock and it virtually unhinged me emotionally for a considerable time. It really is hard to put into words how devastated I was. So many times the people I loved had been taken away from me or left me. I was in a state.

I suppose being busy was not only a relief but also became a kind of therapy. It was certainly more positive than sitting opposite a psychiatrist trying to analyse where everything had gone wrong. The Khartoum trip was fast approaching in September. I couldn't be away from the office for the entire two weeks so I decided to see the group off in Cairo and then return for the second week. Simon, the project manager took over for the first week.

The second week of the Nile adventure was a bit of an eye-opener, even for me. I arrived in Luxor to find Simon on the verge of a breakdown; very upset, extremely agitated and miserably low. Apparently, the demands of the passengers – although most of them pretty trivial – were proving to be a huge burden, to the point that he'd begun to feel everything was his fault. I managed to calm him down, reassure him he was doing well, and when he seemed more relaxed told him of my own personal problems unravelling at home. He seemed better able to put everything into perspective after that.

I was glad I'd decided to join the trip, despite my rather bleak mood. One of the discoveries I made on that journey was the British people's close involvement with their history. One of our evening lectures, given by the Cambridge historian Piers Brendon, was on the role of the navy in the rescue mission. In the course of Piers' presentation, he mentioned the Admiral of the Fleet, at which point one of the passengers put his hand up.

'Did you know he had a younger brother on that campaign?' the gentleman asked.

'Oh yes,' came Piers' prompt reply. 'In fact, he was sent home in disgrace for being under the influence of alcohol once too often.'

'That's not true,' shouted the gentleman, probably wishing he'd never brought the subject up. 'He was returned due to an illness.'

Then, noticing the eyes of the group turning to him in astonishment, he quickly continued: 'I should know – he was my father,' and went on, extremely embarrassed by now, 'he had me very late in life.' And he must have, given that we were celebrating the centenary of the campaign. It turned out that the gentleman in question was an Australian lawyer whose father had not only taken part in the relief expedition but had also been with General Gordon in Khartoum in 1879.

Nothing untoward occurred during the rest of the journey except for a rather amusing incident during the ball we'd arranged at the Cairo Marriot Hotel on the last night. I was seated next to the British ambassador and, not being used to finding myself beside such distinguished company, the first few minutes were only remarkable for their rather awkward silence. I summoned up the courage and, somewhat inanely, asked the ambassador if he'd ever served in Egypt before.

'Oh yes,' he replied, 'but we don't talk about that period.'

My curiosity was immediately piqued: 'And why not?' I enquired.

'That was in 1956,' was his response, followed by a short pause.

'I was sort of on the other side… in the Israeli army,' I chipped in.

After that, and to my surprise, the conversation immediately began to flow; mainly revolving around the rights and wrongs of the war and the current situation in the Middle East, which still hasn't been resolved over thirty years later. We also touched on the lessons learned from the Gordon escapade or, more to the point, the question of whether or not, we do actually learn from other people's mistakes. It made for a very interesting evening.

While I'd been on the Relief of Khartoum trip I'd met and spent time with an American interpreter of Russian and French at the U.N. I was still devastated at separating from Diana. It had only been a few months and although I wasn't expecting or looking for a new relationship it wasn't so surprising that I might inadvertently find solace, and even a new companion. We soon became involved and I embarked on my third marriage. In 1985 the first of our two wonderful boys was born. She was based in Geneva when we met and still worked there when required. One of the most memorable occasions during this period was when I travelled to Switzerland to look after our baby son Jonathan, while she interpreted during Gorbachev's visit to Geneva. On returning home I heard her distinctive voice on the *Nine O'Clock News*.

My next few years at Thomas Cook were spent modernising the company's rather archaic systems, as well as developing new programmes that reflected the travelling public's ever-changing tastes. That's how we found ourselves offering winter sports holidays, and historic tours to the deep south of the United States following in the footsteps of the Civil War. In another of my visits to the Cook archives I discovered that the company had been heavily involved in India during Queen Victoria's reign. I came up with the idea of offering a series of special holidays around the Indian subcontinent, all culminating in Delhi on the same day, to celebrate the centenary of Queen Victoria's golden jubilee of 1887. As part of the preparations we made several trips, in order to check the routes. During one of these we visited the English Country Club in Bangalore, where we were wonderfully looked after. Just before continuing on our way our host stopped us.

'There's something rather special I would like to show you before you leave,' he said before proudly producing a large, heavy and rather worn debtor's ledger. He opened it at a date in 1896. A bold inscription read: 'Lieutenant Winston Churchill still owing 13 rupees'. I offered to repay the debt but was flatly refused.

'What would we show our visitors then?' our host responded.

My last adventure with Thomas Cook was Verdi's *Aida* in May 1987. Sometime earlier that year I'd received a telex sent by a Mr Fawzi Mitwali from, of all places, Vienna. Mr Mitwali was a total stranger and someone I'd never heard of before: 'Would Thomas Cook be interested in selling packages to Egypt which will include performances of *Aida* by the Verona Opera House with Placido Domingo to be staged at the Temple of Luxor?'

My ticket to Aida in Luxor with Placido Dominigo

At first, I thought Mr Mitwali was having a joke but it quickly transpired that it was a serious proposition. An Egyptian living in Vienna, Mr Mitwali was in the final stages of discussions with the Egyptian authorities and their tourist board in order to obtain the necessary permission and, crucially, financial assistance. Both thought the idea was a brilliant way to help revitalise the country's flagging tourist industry. Mr Mitwali assured me that he had obtained the initial agreement from the Verona Opera House for a dozen performances though Placido Domingo had only agreed to sing on the opening night.

The major challenge was being able to persuade potential customers to overcome their lack of faith in Egyptian security and the inevitable high price that such a complex undertaking would demand. On the plus side, this was the first time a performance of one of the most popular operas ever written was to be staged at the actual location where the opera's story takes place. The fact that the first performance of *Aida* had been in Cairo, as part of the celebrations marking the opening of the Suez Canal, gave this new venture additional relevance and sense of adventure. It took me just an hour to reply: 'What a great idea. I'll see how I can promote this wonderful project and get back to you as soon as I've sorted a few things out.'

Of course, there were the inevitable stumbling blocks, the most serious of which was getting the idea past the company's board who weren't too adventurous or, as far as I knew, particularly keen on opera. My solution was to simply bypass them. By the time the project had become public knowledge it was too late for them to opt out.

A short-term success - a long-term big mistake!

As a result of Thomas Cook agreeing to promote *Aida* in Luxor, other European tour operators still hesitating decided to join the fray. It was now a matter of full speed ahead and finding ways of interesting the opera-loving public. My first job was to put together a hasty press release which, to my surprise, produced an immediate response with over six hundred enquiries. The next few months were chaotic. The Empress of India tour was about to go operational while, at the same time, planning for the opera project suddenly became a top priority. Fresh itineraries, incorporating the performance in Luxor, had to be devised and carefully coordinated; aircraft seats and accommodation quickly reserved, and promotional material produced and distributed through the appropriate channels. I was quickly reminded that despite the company owning hundreds of outlets across the UK, staff rarely read the briefing notes from head office. Moreover, most were unlikely to have been to an opera let alone heard of *Aida*. Consequently, we directed publicity material to tour operators specialising in cultural tours and concentrated on bringing out more press releases.

The project was a resounding success. There were over three thousand visitors to Egypt from the UK alone. Many luminaries attended on the first night, including major dignitaries from the Egyptian government, Michael Heseltine with his entourage and of course most of Thomas Cook's senior directors. In order to accommodate people who only wanted to be at the opening night and hear Placido Domingo, and forgo the rest of the tour, we chartered Concorde. Despite the high price, all seats were taken within days.

I have to confess, the opening night was something to behold. On stage, real Egyptian soldiers were arrayed against the backdrop of a dramatic crimson sun setting behind the Nile, as the first notes of the overture rose into a pale pink sky. It was truly awe-inspiring. The atmosphere and setting lifted my spirits. Another adventure, on which so much time and effort had been lavished, was at last coming to fruition. I could sit back, breathe out and enjoy this glorious opera with its wonderful arias, and stop worrying.

In the opera's last scene, the beautiful duet by Radames and Aida while awaiting their death in a pyramid, is one of the most melancholy arias ever written. Listening to it in Luxor, beside the waters of the Nile, left me transported to another world – at least for a short while. I've heard it many times since, but never again has it been surrounded with the same emotional aura.

As it was, it didn't take long for those feelings of wellbeing to evaporate and disappear, as if the event had never happened. Two letters were waiting for me when I got back to my office in the UK. One was from Tim Renton, Foreign Office Minister at the time, inviting me for lunch at Lancaster House; the other was from my boss, asking me to meet him at the Head Office in Berkeley Street. Both appointments were on the same afternoon. I made enquiries at the Foreign Office and discovered that what had prompted the unexpected invitation was the Luxor project's positive impact. Apparently, it had reinvigorated the Egyptian tourist trade and Tim Renton's Egyptian counterpart, Boutros Boutros-Ghali, wanted to meet and thank me personally. It was quite a turn up for the books.

I'd never received an invitation from such an important person or ever stepped foot in Lancaster House.

In Confirmation

In honour of
His Excellency Dr Boutros Boutros-Ghali
Minister of State for Foreign Affairs of the Arab Republic of Egypt

HER MAJESTY'S GOVERNMENT
in the United Kingdom of Great Britain and Northern Ireland
request the honour of the company of

Mr Erich Reich

at Luncheon at Lancaster House St James's SW1
on Monday 11 May 1987 at 12.45 pm for 1 pm
Mr Tim Renton MP
Minister of State for Foreign and Commonwealth Affairs
will preside

*Cars to approach Lancaster House
by way of Cleveland Row*

Enquiries to: Government Hospitality
8 Cleveland Row St James's SW1A 1DH
Telephone: 01-210 4289

Please present this card on arrival

My invitation to Lancaster House

The second appointment was far more sombre, and not wholly unexpected. After all, I was a bit of an outsider in the Thomas Cook hierarchy. I first duly presented myself at Lancaster House, was personally thanked by the man who was later to become Secretary General of the United Nations, chatted to various government officials, Lords and Sirs, and then departed for my second meeting, literally a stone's throw away.

It began something like this: 'Erich, we don't get on too well and it has taken you rather a long time to bring

Thomas Cook Holidays finances back into shape. I think it's probably best we part company.'

It was all very cordial, but no mention was made of the mess I'd found when I'd first arrived, neither was any reference made to the fact that, while not yet perfect, the company's financial base was considerably healthier than before my time. Nor did it take into account the much wider, positive public perception of the company as a result of all the hugely successful projects I'd initiated: The Relief of Khartoum, The Empress of India and Aida in Luxor.

There didn't seem much point in discussing a decision that had probably been made some while back and, anyway, if you're not wanted it's best to take the hint, look forward and seek fresh pastures. Mind you, having a new family with two young children, and being jobless at the age of 52, left me feeling more than a little anxious. When I walked out of the office I was really quite despondent, but I tried desperately to remain positive by continuing to bask in the warm atmosphere I'd experienced at Lancaster House, prior to my sacking.

Chapter Thirteen

My own company Classic Tours - London, aged 52
First Reunion of Kindertransport - London, aged 54
First Charity Bike Ride - Israel, aged 57

If a man will begin with certainties he shall end in doubts
But if he will be content to begin with doubts
He shall end in certainties

Francis Bacon

What next? Good question. I really had no idea where to turn. One moment I was being complimented on a unique achievement, on an emotional high, the next I was bewildered and lost in the fray of looking for work in order to keep a family with two young children - the second having been born in March 1987- above the bread line. What a prospect.

My first step was to secure a good enough financial package from Thomas Cook to allow me some breathing space. Once achieved, I looked at the options open to me. I had ideas and good contacts and realised that part of the reason that Thomas Cook fired me was because I was too entrepreneurial for their liking. So, I decided to set up my own travel company where I wouldn't be answerable to boards of large organisations. I could see a niche for an enterprise that wasn't competing with the large established companies and their rather outdated ways, and was offering something more specialised.

I called my new company Classic Tours. I liked the implication of a historic or literary association that the name suggested. I couldn't have foreseen that it has also lived up to another meaning of 'classic' – of having lasting significance or enduring worth – something I am very proud of.

The problem was I needed start-up funding. The following months proved to be both unsettling and uncertain. Having fallen with a crash from the heights of Thomson's and Thomas Cook to the depths of unemployment, where was I to start my search for financial backing? My first, tentative steps began with an American outfit called Travel South with whom I'd made contact while I was organising the American Civil War tours for Thomas Cook. They agreed to subsidise a brochure for similar tours under the banner of Classic Tours. As it turned out, these trips weren't a huge success, but planning them gave me the space and time to think about other possible ventures. Never to give up had been my attitude for as long as I can remember.

Around the same time, in 1989, I received a letter inviting me to a reunion of the Kindertransport. It may seem odd but up until then I had never really thought about the Kindertransport – in fact I am not even sure how aware I was that I had come on the Kindertransport. After all who would I have discussed it with? As a child it meant nothing. My middle brother Ossie had died at twenty-seven and my older brother Jacques was in Australia. Like so many others who came on the Kindertransport we were just trying to get on with our lives as best we could.

Incredibly, at the reunion I met someone who provided me with an inkling of me at four years old.

On entering the large hall at the Harrow Leisure Centre in Northwest London, I was amazed to be confronted by so many people, the vast majority older than me. As I came into earshot, I realised that the prevailing accents were Germanic. Although the first impression was of a generation and culture different to mine it quickly dawned on me, probably for the first time, that not only did we have the same background but that my misadventures in life were by no means unique.

As the tables were set out with signs of where people went to in England rather than where they came from in Europe, I went to the table for those who had been evacuated at the beginning of the war to Ely in Cambridgeshire. I approached and tentatively enquired whether any of them had known my brother Ossie. A rather stout middle-aged gentleman, a few years older than me, momentarily looked at me and to my amazement said, 'Vye, my boy, you must be his little brother Erich. I remember you both very well.'

'But I was never in Ely,' I exclaimed.

'No, no,' came the immediate response, in a delightful American Yiddish accent. 'We were together on the ship from Gdynia.'

I was absolutely shocked

'What, do you remember of me on the boat?' I enquired.

'Vot, you can't remember?'

'I'm afraid it's a complete blank.'

'All the time running after your brother, crying, shouting, "Ossie, papier, schnell, schnell." Vell, a real pest you were.'

It took time to sink in and to understand what he was saying. I can only assume I had stomach problems which required frequent toilet visits! Not unsurprising, given the trauma of my situation, only four and a world away from the bosom of my mother. I refrained from asking whether I usually made it, with or without paper! Although it did show that I hadn't lost complete control of toilet functions.

Could this early forced self-control have contributed to the fact that I am unable to get drunk, to totally let go? Believe me it's not for lack of trying. Ask my kids. They've made concerted efforts in that direction, hoping no doubt, to discover some hidden skeletons. They should know better. There are plenty of skeletons but all rather visible I'm afraid.

Despite the apparent spectacle I made of myself en route to London I did have my brother Ossie to comfort and look after me; quite a burden for a boy, barely ten, to leave home and look after his four-year-old sibling. Given this was my first sea voyage, it seems such a pity that I can't remember anything about it. Nothing comes to mind, not even the first glimpses of some of those famous landmarks along the River Thames that my children and I have visited on numerous occasions since my inauspicious arrival at the end of August 1939. We were one of the last groups of seventy children, a minute handful, plucked from those millions who perished needlessly and for no other reason than that they were born of the Jewish faith.

Bertha Leverton, herself a Kind, had decided to organise this reunion to mark the Kindertransport's fiftieth anniversary. My curiosity had made me decide to attend and my reply saying I would come also somehow got me involved with the organisation of it. I met the amazing and wonderful Bertha who from that time on dedicated so much of her life to bringing Kinder together and to arranging further reunions. I started to research the Kindertransport and my background in more detail. When I got to hear that Bertha was in urgent need of office space to manage this huge undertaking she had embarked on I was able to help and gave her free office space. This was the beginning of my involvement with the Kindertransport which has continued to this day and of which I am now Chair – although I often think that is only because I am one of the youngest!

But more of this anon. My priority at the time was a livelihood. I remembered Morris Perry, the owner of a small company called Orient Tours who had come to Thomas Cook to see if they'd be interested in buying his pilgrim tour operation. The offer had been declined but I'd remained in touch with the Perry family and thought it might be prudent to contact Morris. After many meetings and much haggling, we made an arrangement for Classic Tours to buy Orient Tours. The purchase didn't turn out to be as fruitful as I'd hoped, but it did provide the platform for the success of the charity challenges operation which I started several years later.

At the same time, I'd also been in touch with the British Museum to see if they'd be interested in archaeological trips for the Friends of the Museum, using some of their curators as on-site lecturers. To my surprise they agreed and, as it turned out, these specialised tours proved pretty successful.

One was a study tour to Egypt during which I was surprised to receive a call from Decca Records. They wanted to get in touch with the renowned opera singer Joan Sutherland who they said was on the trip. I had no idea but on checking the passenger list I saw the name Bonynge, her married name. I contacted my tour manager to ask if he'd find out if she'd be prepared to speak to them.

'Tell them to bugger off,' was Sutherland's reply!

I later discovered that she'd enjoyed herself so much that in Luxor she had persuaded the tour manager, a Dominican priest and opera buff, to let her sit on his lap while she sang arias from *Aida*. He told me that despite her size and weight, hearing her sing at such close proximity was the most wonderful experience. I had organised the itinerary, done the initial recce, made all the arrangements but didn't actually take the tour. Being an opera-lover myself it was a huge disappointment that I missed the chance to meet one of the most famous divas of the twentieth century.

That tour had another special ingredient. I'd managed to contact Sir Steven Runciman, one of the top scholars on the history of the Crusaders. Already in his early eighties, Sir Steven agreed to accompany part of the tour to St Catherine's Monastery on the slopes of Mount Sinai, the same monastery I'd visited with my friends so many years previously, at the end of the war in 1956. Steven Runciman's involvement turned out to be quite a coup. When I informed the senior monks at the Monastery that he'd be one of the group they immediately volunteered to open rooms normally closed to the public.

In 1990, I arranged a trip for the Friends of English National Opera to follow the company during its visit to the Soviet Union, the first major foreign opera company to tour there. ENO's visit had been arranged by Margaret Thatcher as a gesture of good will and took place not long before her departure from prime ministerial office. I joined them in Moscow and will forever recall hearing Verdi's *Macbeth*, sung in English, at the Bolshoi Theatre. I'm not sure I'd recommend visiting Moscow in February; the weather was atrocious, forcing us to battle our way through thick snow with temperatures of -16°.

While organising the ENO tour I'd been put in touch with a lady from Intourist, at that time the only ground-handler with whom foreigners were legally allowed to deal. Just before I was due to return from Moscow this lady asked if I'd like to meet her friend who had an English-speaking boyfriend. 'Of course,' I immediately responded. She then told me, 'His name is 'Robert... Robert Heifetz.' Noticing my dubious expression she added, 'Yes Jascha Heifetz's son.'

I was amazed. Jascha Heifetz has always been one of my favourite violinists and I have more than twenty of his recordings. Robert, I discovered, was a truly delightful and gentle man. He lived in San Francisco, where he and his Russian girlfriend were later married. We became quite friendly and visited them several years later. Robert told me how his parents had met. Heifetz had flown to Texas to give a concert. On arriving he'd been met by a crowd of cheering people. Much to his disappointment he discovered that the crowd weren't there for him but for Florence Arto, a famous silent film actress then married to the film producer King Vidor. Heifetz met Florence and it didn't take long for him to woo, seduce and marry her. Robert was one of their two children.

When I asked Robert whether he ever travelled with his father, he told me he'd done so only once, to Israel in 1953. As part of the concert, Heifetz had played a short piece by Richard Strauss. At the time Strauss was considered to be a Nazi composer and his works were unofficially banned in Israel. Heifetz felt that music was above these matters and was adamant that he would play what he wanted. After one recital Heifetz was attacked. He left Israel and did not return until 1970.

Behind the scenes, the small matter of sorting out finance for Classic Tours to purchase Orient Tours was going on. I negotiated a personal loan from the bank, using my house as security. It wasn't what I ideally wanted to do but I had no choice. Worse was to come as several months later I discovered I'd been misled, and realised that the volume of business had been exaggerated and the overhead costs minimised. I have to take some of the blame for this blunder. I really should have looked more closely into the company's figures and finances but it never occurred to me that a family I'd known for so long would misrepresent the facts.

Orient Tours were responsible for quite a few pilgrim tours to the Holy Land. In Israel the ground-handling was done by a company Perry had set up for his daughter and son-in-law. As part of the purchase agreement I was required to use that company but their charges were exorbitant. It was a commitment I couldn't get out of and one that kept Classic Tours on a financial knife edge. While we managed to sustain the costs under normal conditions it proved a burden too far when the going began to get tough.

The inevitable eventually happened in 1991, precipitated by the Gulf War. It's not hard for me to recall lonely walks through the empty streets of Tel Aviv, with Scud missiles randomly floating across the sky overhead and no tourists or pilgrims in sight. It was just one of those hurdles that suddenly appear from nowhere, have to be negotiated and the consequences appraised. I returned to the UK wondering if and how this particular problem could indeed be resolved.

It all depended on how long we'd be able to survive with no new bookings and cancelled tours, but with the same overheads. I managed to hold on for a couple of months before it became apparent that, with debts piling up and no money coming in, Classic Tours wasn't going to survive for much longer. Following discussions with accountants and solicitors, I came to the decision that the best course of action was to go into voluntary liquidation. At the time there were only three groups booked, all of which had been paid for, so I wasn't letting anyone down. It was a terribly sad moment; first having to tell the staff that they no longer had jobs and then, once they'd left, wandering through an eerie, dark, empty office. I felt so lonely and depressed; once again circumstances had conspired to put a major obstacle in my way. I had little alternative but to start yet again. Most urgently, I had to find a way of bringing in an income in order to feed the family and, at the same time, service the bank loan guaranteed against our home.

A dearest friend Mike (he knows who I mean) and family – including Auntie Irene and my nephew David – helped me over the immediate financial crisis. Stuart at Peltours had decided to take over Orient Tours from the liquidator on the basis that I became a part-time consultant for the pilgrim market. He also agreed to cover future ventures I wanted to organise under Peltours' travel licence. Finally, my landlord, Maurice let me keep the office for several months, rent free. It's at times of crisis that you find out who your true friends are, who really care for you and are prepared to help you, despite not knowing what the final outcome might be and I owe them all a huge debt of gratitude. Together with my one remaining, loyal member of staff, Linda, I managed to get through that horrendous period.

I spent two days a week at Peltours, helping them rebuild a pilgrims' market, while spending the rest of the time sorting out the never-ending issues that seemed to be confronting us in preparation for a very different venture. **This was a fund-raising bicycle challenge in Israel.**

I am putting this in bold because it changed my life and those of many others. It created a new way of supporting charity. But it's difficult to remember just how and when I came up with the idea.

Given my background it was partly to do with what was happening in Israel. During my walks in a deserted Tel Aviv, the terrible effect of bombs, conflicts and never-ending wars in the Middle East past and present haunted me. The thought of being able to do something positive for that war-torn region undoubtedly sowed some seeds. I suppose this was combined with my natural instinct to help those less fortunate than myself. I had had a taste of fund-raising challenges when I ran the marathon. However, the final spur was Maurice, my close friend of many years whose daughter was, and still is, a resident at Ravenswood, a Jewish residential village for people with severe special needs. Whenever we met, Maurice would invariably ask me, 'Johnny isn't there anything you can do with travel to help raise funds for Ravenswood, something that could raise significant amounts?'

Given the circumstances I found myself in, following the liquidation of my company, I didn't need much persuasion. It was simply a case of being able to come up with a good idea; something different that would appeal to the Jewish community who supported Ravenswood. I decided that whatever idea I came up with, it would take place in Israel. I wanted to encourage new visitors to Israel, to show the country in a different light. And so, I came up with the idea of a five-day, 400-kilometre cycle In Israel. I decided on cycling because it allowed the possibility of seeing so much more than if trekking. It would be a serious physical challenge which would hopefully inspire people to take part and persuade others to support them in what would be a very difficult endeavour.

I approached Ravenswood and they decided very quickly to go for it. But I was nervous that they wouldn't get enough participants. So, I approached the Edinburgh Medical Missionary Society (EMMS) whom I knew well from operating their pilgrim trips to Israel. They supported a Christian Arab hospital in Nazareth so I was confident that a project in Israel would appeal to them. I went to Edinburgh, explained the concept and told them that it would be with Ravenswood (and who they were). I also pointed out that as well as seeing holy sites there would be an opportunity to visit the hospital they supported in Nazareth. They also very quickly decided to go for it!

So, I had two charities signed up, one supporting a project in the UK and one supporting a project in Israel. A group that would consist of Jewish and Christian participants was a very important aspect to me and to the possible success of this unusual project.

Somehow the Gulf War, with its Desert Shield title and references to the Old Testament, led me to the idea of a biblical bike ride from Dan to Beersheba; a ride that would start and finish at the edges of the ancient Israelite kingdom within which, historical evidence suggests, King David collected his taxes. The concept produced an immediate and positive reaction from both charities.

All that remained was to create an itinerary, find accommodation, bicycles, mechanics, doctors and who knows what else! Numerous telexes and phone messages to bicycle shops and ground-handlers in Israel yielded nothing. Then, one day, we received a short message from a small bike shop in Jerusalem, run by a man called Chaim Rockman, saying that he had a few bikes, was a fully-fledged bike guide and that he might be able to help us.

Brochure for first charity bike ride 1992

Subsequent discussions led to communication with the Israeli travel company, Ayala Tours. Much later I discovered that both these contacts thought I was slightly unhinged, wondering why anybody would want to cycle for five days in Israel, most of the time trying to dodge impatient Israeli drivers. They didn't think I'd ever be able to persuade the fifty or so cyclists that I'd told them I'd be recruiting to participate in this outlandish enterprise. It took several visits to Israel, checking out possible routes and getting stuck in the mud somewhere in the lower hills of Galilee, to come up with a reasonable itinerary.

It soon became apparent that rather than fifty, there would be over two hundred participants! We were in shock and it raised the small matter of being able to find enough bicycles. As far as I could work out, Chaim had no more than forty at his disposal but finally, after a lot of begging and scraping, I managed to secure enough, albeit a rather motley assortment of bikes.

Then there were the mechanics, tour guides, and doctors to recruit. And most importantly for the participants, accommodation to organise – all essential ingredients for the smooth running of such a huge new venture. Although from the outset smooth running didn't seem likely.

Before we'd even left the UK there was minor chaos at Heathrow as members of the group rushed from one end of the terminal to the other looking for tickets, mislaid luggage or family members who'd come to see them off. And they all seemed intent on arguing with the poor airline staff: 'I must sit next to so and so,' or, 'I can't possibly sit next to that person.' I quickly realised that our best laid plans for the sleeping arrangements were probably doomed.

Somehow, we managed to get the entire group past bewildered El Al staff and onto the flight without too long a delay, leaving streams of tears flowing from friends and family back in the airport. I can still hear the words of warning: 'Be careful, don't fall off your bike, eat properly and don't forget to phone the moment you land.' You would have been forgiven if you'd thought that these were young children embarking on a trip to the Gobi desert, and that they'd never travelled before.

Our arrival at Ben Gurion Airport was met with unexpected delays. These were mainly as a result of people who'd either mislaid or forgotten to renew their passports, or, despite having been given strict instructions, hadn't filled in their entry forms correctly.

And so, on November 21st,1992, somehow, my 'team' were gathered at Kibbutz Dan ready to welcome our large and rather apprehensive group for the start of the first ever overseas Charity Bicycle Challenge.

Four hours later, five coaches entered the gates of Kibbutz Dan in the northern Hills of Galilee, depositing over two hundred bleary-eyed, hungry and very tired would-be cyclists. A mad rush to the dining room ensued, the entire group demanding to be served with hot cups of coffee and something to eat immediately. It was a real Jewish affair, with everyone worrying that the food would run out before their turn – which, of course, it didn't. As you might expect, the EMMS contingent waited quietly in the queue for their turn with hardly a murmur.

Slowly but surely, as most of the group settled down to the serious business of filling their stomachs, a kind of order was established and the noise level subsided. It was a lull before the storm of handing out keys to the rooms. Somehow, everybody seemed to have forgotten what arrangement they'd asked for in their original request. Having finally established where everyone would be sleeping the time came for bike fitting – another delicate hurdle to be overcome before nightfall.

You can discover a lot about human nature when trying to please so many people, all at the same time – what suits one person seems to enrage another. By the end of the day – and before having even cycled an inch – the management team, the mechanics, the tour managers and, I daresay, many members of the kibbutz were shattered. What had I let myself in for?

Just after midnight, as more and more tired human beings gave in and allowed sleep to take over, peace descended. I lay on my bed next to my two exhausted little boys, Jonathan, aged seven, and Joel, just five years old, my mind in absolute turmoil. As I looked at their quiet sleeping faces, for once not asking me a myriad of awkward questions, I began to wonder whether any of us would last the distance; five days and four hundred kilometres spent looking after a bunch of demanding Northwest London inhabitants of my ilk, together with a smaller number of much quieter, and far less demanding born-and-bred Christian Scots.

My alarm rang just as dawn began to appear on the horizon. It felt as if I'd just fallen asleep but in truth I had managed about three hours of undisturbed slumber. I stumbled from door to door trying to wake up the would-be cyclists only to be met with groans – 'It's too early, go away, I'm not ready to get up, I don't need any breakfast.'

It took several rounds with my dreaded, rather loud megaphone, warning all that they'd miss breakfast and that we were leaving as planned at nine o'clock, with or without those not yet ready for the message to get through. The same message they'd be forced to hear over the next five mornings! What a sight – over two hundred bedraggled characters schlepping huge suitcases onto a lorry. Helping load their baggage, I had to wonder what on earth they'd brought with them. It seemed like most of their suitcases were filled with enough clothes to last for two months rather than a week.

Miraculously, we managed to set off only half an hour later than planned. Of course, no sooner had we departed and were on our way, than I was informed of various items that had been inadvertently left behind. The most memorable was someone who'd brought his own bike along with a new spare wheel, which he'd locked to a tree branch then promptly forgotten until his first puncture around lunchtime. Unfortunately, he also managed to mislay the key so, as far as I'm aware, his spanking new wheel is still in that tree; albeit slightly weather-beaten by now.

My first lesson was to try to understand how a group of grown up adults – most with families and children, many highly trained professionals and quite a few running their own profitable companies – had suddenly become child-like: 'Erich, how many more miles?' 'Why are there so many hills?' 'Where can I put my bike?' 'I can't find my helmet.' 'I'm thirsty.' 'I'm hungry.' There seemed no end to the questions. On top of these, I was overwhelmed by a never-ending stream of complaints; mostly thankfully pretty minor. It took me a few hours to acknowledge the metamorphosis that had taken place before realising that I had to treat some of the participants in their new guise of spoilt children rather than adults. I'd suddenly become the father, headmaster and communal leader all rolled into one, and was supposed to have an answer for everything. It wasn't at all what I had expected.

With two participants on Scope Red Sea Challenge 1997

Meanwhile, I was travelling in a van at the back of the group with both my boys beside me asking for information about the smallest detail of everything we passed. I really didn't have time to answer. I had to find ways to keep them occupied so I could concentrate on keeping two hundred cyclists on the move, and allay the numerous fears that so many suddenly seemed to have become afflicted with, as we descended from the Hills of Galilee toward the Sea of

Galilee. At the water stops I got the boys to help fill the fast-emptying water bottles. It was great fun for them, particularly as much of the water ended up on the ground, and they really enjoyed the fuss that was made of them.

My first serious mistake happened during the lunch stop. One of the Ravenswood residents who'd come on the challenge was unable to carry on so I volunteered to take his bike and cycle to Ein Gev, our evening stop. Before setting off, I explained to Vivienne, the Ravenswood representative, that she should go ahead but under no circumstances allow any changes to the rooming list. The boys, meanwhile, stayed in the van with the Ayala Tour representative Yair, learning a few words of Hebrew en route.

When I arrived at Ein Gev I found all hell had broken loose. Vivienne's lovely soft nature meant by the time the first half a dozen or so cyclists had arrived the list of rooming arrangements had become useless. Everyone seemed to have either forgotten or had changed their minds as to who they were going to share a room with. It was an unmitigated mess, taking until well after midnight to sort out and calm down all the hungry, tired and vociferous cyclists. There I was, standing in total darkness; my two boys clinging to my legs, virtually asleep, with their mother complaining loudly that I should have sorted them out first. She probably had a point. What a fantastic and memorable first day.

We learned lessons very quickly: no more changes to the rooming list, no cycling for me, and the need for regular and very voluble reminders to all cyclists not to stray into the middle of the road else they were very likely to be hit by an impatient Israeli driver, even on the quiet roads we were using. Quite how we managed to escape any serious accidents was a real miracle. Maybe it was the make-up of these amazing two groups that called down God's blessing and, more importantly, gave us his protection.

Of course, there were some who had to take the odd break and travel in a vehicle and others who got minor scrapes and bruises. At the same time, given the competitive nature of many of the Ravenswood participants there was plenty of rivalry between the men as to who could cycle the fastest, despite the constant reminder that we weren't taking part in a race but in a challenge to raise funds for charity. I suppose it's only natural that boys will be boys, never mind their age and the potential consequences. For many participants the challenges of the adventure provided an escape from the tensions of regular life, be they family issues or business matters.

We finished in Beersheba; the biblical city of Abraham and Jacob, the largest town in the south of Israel and the last post before the Negev Desert. Virtually all the participants made it to the end; rightly feeling well proud. One of the most amazing features of Ravenswood bike rides from the outset was the inclusion of some residents as participants, most of whom had never been abroad before. To see them cope, even with carers, not only with cycling but the demands of staying in a different place every night, different food, packing, unpacking, the climate and all the other challenges was humbling. They were always honoured at the end of ride celebration and to see how proud they were of what they had achieved was just as important as the funds raised. The two charities together on this first bike ride raised the fantastic sum of £600,000. Many had made new friends and the majority had surpassed physical barriers they never thought possible. They'd all got to learn, in some detail, about the two charities for which the funds were being raised. Above all, the entire group finished on an extraordinary high, praising one another on their unique achievement in being part of the first overseas Charity Bicycle Challenge.

Chapter Fourteen

Twenty years of Classic Tours, aged 57 -77
Twenty years of the Kindertransport

I expect to pass through life but once,
if therefore there can be any kindness I can show,
any good thing I can do to any fellow being,
let me do it now
and not defer as I shall not pass this way again.

William Penn

At the time of planning the first charity bike ride in Israel I never thought of it beyond a one-off venture. I was overwhelmed on my return from Israel and realised I had come up with a concept with potential, although I could never have foreseen just how great that might be. Here was a possible new direction for me. The idea of being able to provide an opportunity for people to challenge themselves physically, while at the same time making a difference to those who are unable to help themselves, took hold of me. Maybe also somewhere within my subconscious, the idea of giving back to the country that had saved me was lurking. Suffice to say, I considered the concept worthwhile, and one that required further development. I was excited by the new horizons I could discover by using my experiences in travel to provide an innovative platform for raising funds for charity, as well as allowing me to overcome some of my own personal inhibitions.

Just after completing the first bike ride, a charity worker from a local British Heart Foundation branch came into our office asking if we could make a donation to their charity. We weren't able to donate very much so I suggested that it might be financially more beneficial to try a charity bike challenge abroad. The idea had never crossed their mind, and I only suggested it on the spur of the moment. Imagine my surprise when a few days later we received a call from their head office asking for a meeting. We'd just recruited our third charity, and initiated another bike challenge in the Holy Land.

Meanwhile, our first two charities had asked if we could organise separate challenges for each of their individual organisations. I think that the idea of kosher food and resting on the Sabbath on the one hand, and fish only on Fridays on the other didn't sit well together, not to speak of the foibles each of the charities' participants had demonstrated during the first challenge. I suppose praying from both the Old and the New Testament, at more or less the same time, must have added to the confusion. The following year we had three bike challenges, all in Israel.

Bike rides always yielded unexpected experiences. During the EMMS challenge there was a rainstorm in Jerusalem which caused a flash flood down into the Dead Sea, washing away the only road between Ein Gedi and Masada. This called for some quick thinking by myself and Yair while we arranged a transfer to the other side of Jerusalem. We rejigged the itinerary and accommodation and even provided time out for some of the participants to float on the famous mineral-laden waters of the Dead Sea underneath a clear blue sky, an experience much cherished by the participants and happily putting any changes to the original plans, out of mind. While we were waiting one of the participants who had been on the first bike ride the year before asked me, 'Erich, are there any differences between our group and Ravenswood?'

I considered the question for a moment. 'Well, actually there are a few but to try and sum it up, you lot all bring cameras and take pictures of every holy site you encounter. The other lot also bring cameras, but they take pictures of each other,' I replied.

With a staggering 290-plus participants, the 1993 Ravenswood challenge that year turned out to be one of the largest single groups we ever had. At the end of it I vowed never again to have such a large group. Imagine all those British Jews, many from North London, descending on a lovely, quiet hotel in Ashkelon, on the shores of the Mediterranean. In an age before mobile phones and emails we were inundated with hundreds of telexes and phone messages from worried relatives. To complicate matters, my two young sons and their mother were with me again. So, once more I had both family and group management problems to cope with at one and the same time.

The torrential rain that fell from the skies on the first morning did remind the nervous participants that they were involved in a real challenge. What a sight hundreds of cyclists battling against wind and streaming rain, most with black bin bags over their heads. Watching them depart, I couldn't help wondering how many would reach our final destination, 450 kilometres away and what shape they'd be in when they got there.

Meanwhile, according to his mother, my youngest, Joel, had a high temperature and wasn't able to travel. I called a doctor and agreed to leave behind a much-needed vehicle with strict instructions to follow as soon as possible. We eventually managed to get all the cyclists on the road, with the distance between the first and last ever-increasing. Thankfully the rain cleared, leaving a cloud of steam wafting above the throng of cyclists as the deluge that had fallen on them evaporated. Imagine my surprise when, a couple of hours into the ride, all chirpy and raring to go, Joel appeared with his mother. Perhaps it was just the rain that had afflicted him– who knows?

As the days progressed there were plenty of bruises and numerous complaints. 'Erich, you didn't tell us there were so many hills.' 'The distances are all wrong – I've just checked my speedometer and you're at least a mile out.' And so it went on for five days. I recall there were two rather notable incidents. The first took place while we were camped for the night at Makhtesh Ramon (the Ramon Crater) in the Negev Desert. Most of the cyclists were shattered and already asleep when the high-pitched tone of one of our field phones rose sharply above the assorted snoring cadenzas. Since the voice on the line was speaking in Hebrew I was handed the phone. It was the Israeli police enquiring whether a Mr something-or-other was with the group. I assured the officer that indeed he was and asked if the message was important as he was fast asleep. 'Tell him his au pair is looking for him,' was his short answer. I didn't ask for the details, I simply informed the person in question. I never did find out the reason for the message, or the outcome!

The second incident occurred the next day, which just happened to be the day when I'd planned to cover the longest distance. As usual I was at the back of the group when I got a phone message from one of the cyclists at the front – a member of the fast 'black' group – complaining that they were at the lunch stop but there was no lunch in sight. Given that the food transport vehicle hadn't even passed me at the back I was aware that tensions must be rising fast up at the front. After all, food is always fundamental in the Jewish culture and certainly no different on a bike ride! Fortuitously, at that very moment the food transport vehicle whizzed past me. I suggested that the group carry on about ten kilometres or so to the next wadi, assuring them that when they arrived they'd find lunch waiting. Luckily it was or I'd have probably been lynched.

Our last stop, before reaching the finishing line in Eilat, was in the Timna Valley at a place known as King Solomon's Pillars, or King Solomon's Mines, located some twenty-five kilometres north of Eilat. Apparently, the valley was mined for copper from as far back as the times of the Egyptian Pharaoh, Ramses. There's also evidence suggesting that Solomon tried to get as much copper from this area as he could, in order to help fund his wooing of the Queen of Sheba. Whatever took place in the past, it's a beautiful region in the middle of a red-hued desert, a wonderful spot for a final few moments of relaxation, and a sandwich or two washed down with some tepid water, before the last tiring stretch of sweaty cycling.

It seems inevitable that wherever you stop in Israel you're confronted with history dating back thousands of years. You might wish that somehow you could be transported along the waves of time to be deposited amongst the ancient Egyptians, Hebrews or Nomads, in order to understand what life was like way back in the mists of our ancestors' eras. But these are only fleeting fancies, quickly banished by an aching backside and the thought of the finishing line followed by a shower, food and a proper bed to sleep in. We arrived at our destination to be greeted by raucous cheers, plenty of drinks and reunions with family members who'd flown from home to greet their cycling heroes.

The Charity Challenges' final night parties have often included an auction of some of the many items people have lost or forgotten en route. During one of these events the charity's representative, who happened to be a very good looking lady, decided to auction her bra which, I should add, she hadn't mislaid or lost en route. What can I say – given that the majority of participants were male her charity benefited from considerable additional funds that she raised.

By the end of that Challenge I was absolutely exhausted, I'd never felt so tired, both mentally and physically. It's impossible to describe the difficulties involved, and the patience required, in moving a group of nearly three hundred for five days over 450 kilometres. They never stopped describing in detail their aches and pains or, above all, loudly voicing their complaints. Having said that, all was forgotten and everything forgiven once everyone had soaked under a shower, eaten a decent Friday evening meal, and drifted to sleep knowing that they wouldn't be woken by me at the crack of dawn. On top of the exhilaration of surviving the challenge, the group had also raised huge sums for Ravenswood. As Shakespeare, in his wisdom, quite rightly pointed out: 'All's well that ends well.'

Inevitably many incidents have occurred in the intervening years between that second bike challenge in 1993 and more recent times. There have been far too many to describe in this book, so I'll just mention the few that stand out for me. During one challenge, while we were staying on a kibbutz in the north of Israel, a couple who were both married, but not to each other, decided to sleep in a two-person tent instead of in the school building with the rest of the group. Obviously intrigued, two young kibbutz children came up to me and asked what the pair was up to and if it would be okay to join them. Fortunately, after several minutes and a few tactful words I was able to dissuade them.

During another bike ride, this time in Egypt, two participants became intimately involved within a day or so of our setting out. Being at the back of the group I couldn't help but notice romance as it blossomed. Unfortunately, there was a problem. The young lady involved was married and her husband was due to arrive to meet her on the last day as the group was departing for home. A very interesting situation presented itself at the airport; frantic kisses, hugs and tears for the departing lover followed by similar welcoming emotions for the incoming husband.

I'm hardly likely to forget the group cycling in Jordan. When the ground-handler's lorry got stuck in the sands of Wadi Rum he refused to continue, never mind there were still two days of cycling ahead, or that I had nearly one hundred tired, irritable cyclists wishing to continue. Anyway, after much haggling and a lot of sweat – mainly mine and the participants' – we managed to push the lorry back out onto the road. The following year I decided to use a different ground-handler and when I arrived at Petra the owner of the local company I'd used the previous year was waiting for me, shouting and hurling abuse. We had to call the police to calm him down. It wasn't something I'd expected would be part of organising overseas charity challenges.

About ten years ago, during one of our bike challenges in Israel, we stopped for a lunch break near Kibbutz Ein Harod; while we were there a group of youngsters passed by. When I found out they were from the Kibbutz I tentatively enquired if they knew Michael Odem, who'd been in the army with me. There was a short pause and one of the children looked at me innocently, 'You mean Michael, a member of our old veterans?'

What could I say? There I was cycling the length and breadth of Israel, to be brought up sharply by a young boy and told that at sixty-five I was an old veteran. Time, it appears, stops for no one. But it did bring it home to me that earning my living was not that easy. I spent part of my time in the office coming up with ideas and itineraries, meeting with charities, organising all the elements required and trying to make sure that the company was at least breaking even which for the first few years it did not do. But I also had to take the groups, cycle, be away from my young family and it was often far from easy.

We were, of course, very quickly copied by other companies. Something we had to get used to over the years – I suppose such is the price of innovation.

A few years earlier we had decided to widen our charity challenge horizons and check out China. I went to investigate if we could organise a trek that included the Great Wall. Before flying out I explained to the local ground-handler, in minute detail, what we were looking for. They duly met me at Beijing airport and, after driving several miles out of the Chinese capital, stopped on a major road with heavy traffic. I was informed that this is where we would start the trek. It took several hours explaining that we didn't want to walk on a main road but on pathways and tracks, preferably through the hills, to the Great Wall. To be fair they learned fast. Since then many very successful treks and bike challenges have taken place in China.

Mind you, China is an extraordinary country of contrasts. On the one hand, you have the huge conurbations of Beijing, Shanghai, and several other large cities with populations of over ten million inhabitants, and where all the latest modern conveniences are available. On the other, there are small villages along the Yellow River, where millions of people live in caves, albeit with electricity and, of course, the obligatory television. On one of my first recces I was introduced to the local mayor in her home on the shores of the mighty Yellow River. She lived in a fairly spacious cave where we were treated to wonderful Chinese tea and local cakes. I was told that some ten million Chinese still lived that way.

Taking groups to the USA was interesting. You might imagine a modern and civilised country where operating a trek or bike ride wouldn't create any undue problems, particularly since there's no apparent language issue. Not so! On my first recce around the Grand Canyon I discovered that the Midwest more or less shuts down with sunset, and if you haven't eaten before you'll probably have to wait for breakfast which will, admittedly, duly be served in huge quantities. Despite having obtained with some difficulty the many police permits required for our first group to America of fifty-to-sixty cyclists, I received an urgent phone call from the tour manager informing me that they were at the entrance of the Grand Canyon but that the local rangers wouldn't let them in without a Canyon Ranger's Permit, and that they weren't interested in our police permits. A couple of hours' negotiations later the group were allowed in, but four at a time at five-minute intervals.

We may think that in the UK we have very bureaucratic and ineffective processes but as one travels around the globe, trying to organise unusual itineraries, one quite quickly discovers that other countries' idiosyncrasies are frequently far more convoluted than ours.

On another trip to China our Bike Challenge went through territory rarely visited by foreigners, finishing at the site of the Terracotta Warriors. During my first recce we had decided to use a hotel along the route. While terms were being negotiated by my friends, who were local to the area, I was advised to stay in the car. I was under strict instructions not to get out, and to make myself as inconspicuous as possible. While sitting there, waiting for their return, it dawned on me that this probably spelt trouble. My misgivings were justified! After the group had arrived and begun their journey into the unknown, I was woken in the early hours of the morning and told that all their passports had been confiscated, never mind that we had the relevant permits from Beijing. When I raised this I was told, 'We are not in Beijing. Here different rules apply.' Not really 'rules' – simply more dollars and in cash. We settled on $50 per person.

Over the years we operated several bike rides in the old Soviet Union and subsequently in Russia. One of these was a challenge from St Petersburg to Moscow, organised for Friends of Russian Children who supported a children's hospital burns unit in Moscow. Scanning the participants' list before we set out I noticed the name Carol Thatcher, daughter of Maggie, who turned out to be a most capable cyclist and a very lively character. When we arrived in Moscow I was informed that someone (Carol) had arranged for the group to have tea at the British Embassy. Walking around the beautiful building, replete with exquisite paintings in every room, Carol said to me, 'On my last visit here I was with my mother, and my brother and sister-in-law but the latter two seemed more interested in shopping in the not very exciting State Department Store Gum than taking the opportunity to visit the wonderful museums and galleries dotted around the city.'

I became friends with Carol who did quite a few charity challenges with us. In 1997 Carol sent me a copy of *Below the Parapet*, her biography of her father, Denis and in which she wrote to me: 'The tale of another Thatcher, with a different "on your bike" link!'

It was only after I'd visited the hospital the charity was raising funds for in Russia, that I realised that most of the burns weren't from fires but as a result of boiling water. Partly as a result of carelessness, these burns were caused by the rather primitive cooking facilities and samovars that were available back then. The wards were full of children suffering from varying degrees of burns with terrible pain that became all too apparent, and very real, when we heard the loud wails and cries emanating from wards. After our visit, the entire group realised that raising the funds had been worth all the soreness, aches and bites; cycling over five hundred kilometres along terrible roads, sandy paths, often having to fight their way through hordes of ferocious midges.

On another Russian bike challenge the local tour leader, Ilya, who normally cycled in the front, suddenly decided to join me at the back.

'Is anything the matter?' I enquired.

'The police are providing security until we reach our next evening stop,' he replied.

'So why have you moved back here?' I responded

'The further I am from the police the better,' Ilya said

Although this was sometime after the demise of the Soviet Union the police menace still hung heavily over the Jewish community.

Iceland is another fascinating country. For a start, much of it could be described as a cold desert with black lava sand, rather than the yellow type found in the Sahara. You cycle along desolate lava-strewn tracks, past mountains that are either about to erupt or which have done so recently. Usually it's pretty windy, which was the case on our first bike challenge there. Our itinerary took us on a circular route. At one point, due to the wind, it was an effort not to get blown over sideways. After this it took half an hour to cycle a mile uphill against the wind and then, holding on for dear life, it became a struggle to stay upright and not get blown over to the other side, but then the pay-off; cycling over twenty kilometres with the wind at our backs and no need to touch the pedals all the way. Having reached the last bridge we had to cross a couple of miles from our night stop, we were told that due to the strong winds the bridge had been closed. A transfer by coach became the order of the day. Talk about being at the right place but at the wrong time!

In 1997, I was taking a challenge with a hundred or so participants cycling along the Nile from Luxor to Aswan. We were about an hour south of Luxor when I got a message on my mobile from the office in London telling me that a group of terrorists had just shot some tourists at Luxor's famous archaeological site. The news caused mayhem, not so much with the cyclists but at HQ in the UK. To be fair, the pictures shown on the news were pretty gruesome and I can quite understand why the charity wanted everyone back home before another incident occurred. Truth be told, though, cycling ever-further away from where the shootings had taken place, we were probably quite safe. Anyway, we arranged a special flight from Aswan the following day, after only one day's cycling.

Natural calamities have been the ones that have hit us most frequently. The very first trek in China started with heavy rains washing away the tracks we were supposed to be trekking on. To add to the discomfort, most of the tents leaked, resulting in a great number of wet, hungry and irritated trekkers. The saving grace was that this particular trek was linked to participants getting to see a live performance of Puccini's opera *Turandot* in the Forbidden City of Beijing, at the end of the trek. The anguish and suffering of the first few days was quickly forgotten.

Our most complicated venture was undoubtedly the one we organised for the Marie Curie Hospices of which Edwina Currie was a driving force. There were five separate itineraries, all finishing in Warsaw. Surprisingly, not everyone was aware that Marie Curie was Polish and not French. The five starting points were Berlin, Prague, Krakow, Gdansk and Vilnius. All told, over four hundred cyclists took part. By staggering the starting days, all the groups managed to finish in front of what had been the Joseph Stalin Palace of Culture and Science – now just the Palace of Culture and Science – within three hours of each other. It was a wonderful sight, each group, with different coloured tee-shirts, singing and shouting as they gathered at the steps of the building. The cyclists had raised over £1 million for the charity.

Whether cycling, trekking, mountain climbing or running, the challenges have a deep effect on their participants. Prior to taking part in a challenge many have never ventured forth on a bicycle, slept under canvas or had to hide behind a boulder to relieve themselves! For many it has been a voyage of discovery to realise the extent of their own endurance, to learn that it was OK to rely on others, to help others to complete the challenge, as well as trying to understand the different cultures of the host countries in which the challenges have taken place. They have produced a long-surviving camaraderie amongst people who had never met prior to the challenge they were involved with. Each challenge has proved that hardships are easier to deal with when we are surrounded by like-minded individuals. Each challenge has afforded time to perhaps forget pressures and day-to-day problems at home and instead concentrate on completing a very demanding endeavour for a very good cause.

It had been quite a struggle in the early years trying to get my company on an even financial keel. But somehow, we had got there and it was such a good feeling. But for me personally it was still difficult. I was trying to repay the hefty personal loan I had taken from the bank to buy the business. By the mid-Nineties I knew that my marriage was again in trouble and I moved into a rented flat near Highgate. I would never have been able to make ends meet if Auntie had not been there to help me. She was there when I needed help and I thank her from the bottom of my heart.

I was again on my own but was very involved, on a daily basis, with my two young boys, taking them to school, swimming, piano or violin lessons or the myriad other activities they were involved in. I was also travelling a lot with the groups. But it seemed fate was about to strike again. It was 1996 and Ravenswood were going to Egypt. It was a dilemma whether or not to go with this group of over one hundred cyclists and be away from the boys, then aged nine and eleven, knowing that I'd be abroad, on and off, for a period of two months. The alternative was to abandon the charity. This was something I couldn't really contemplate doing. So off I traipsed to Luton airport where a young lady greeted me with a lovely smile.

'Hello Erich,' she said in a broad Scottish accent.

After looking at her quizzically for a moment I responded, 'I remember your face but can't for the life of me recall your name.'

It didn't seem like a good start. She had every right to feel miffed but I'm not sure she was. On the trip, we enjoyed good chats at the museum in Cairo and the pyramids. She had been a participant on the Ravenswood Challenge the previous year in Israel, along with about fifteen others from Glasgow, and I recalled later having talked to her at some length during one of our evening stops. She had also been notable on that event for being the last and very late arrival at the starting point, along with her own bike and her friend Michael. I did, however, note that she seemed rather young and, having made an agreement with myself not to get attached to anyone younger than my oldest offspring, the issue didn't warrant any further thoughts in that direction.

Well, by the end of her second challenge, four hundred kilometres and five days later, I'd discovered that she was indeed older than my firstborn and that she might be interested in further communication. Why else would she have given me her phone number? She even gave me the impression that should I ever find myself in Scotland she'd be delighted to hear from me. After numerous phone calls, from places as far apart as Jordan, Egypt and Russia, I eventually found an excuse to visit Scotland. And the rest as they say is history. I think it wasn't a specific moment of discovery but the numerous previous experiences that led to our mutual attraction. For a start, we had met a year earlier, but at that point Linda was grieving the loss of her parents and I was still involved with my previous family. So many disappointments in the past had contributed to an insecurity which made me rather wary and question if this one would succeed. Had I found a partner who instinctively wished to give as well as receive? It took the two bike challenges, a year apart, to start the process, with all the emotional hurdles involved, and to believe that this venture might just work.

Linda and I have been together ever since. Linda commuted between Glasgow and London for a long period and eventually moved to London to be with me. Our wedding in 2003 by the sea at Turnberry in Scotland, was a very special day for us. As we stood under the chupah our friends Max and Louise had organised, surrounded by family and friends including my brother Jacques who came all the way from Australia specially, I felt content.

I suppose the after-effect of that first Kindertransport reunion was to move me into trying to discover what happened to my parents. Numerous letters to various organisations holding archive data yielded the information that my father was in Auschwitz as late as 1944. I could not find out anything more about what happened to my mother. She either died in the Warsaw Ghetto or was taken to Treblinka – I will never know.

I have visited Vienna several times and on each occasion, have gone to its famous Central Cemetery on the outskirts of the city. It is one of the largest cemeteries in the world and a rather beautiful place, full of trees and greenery. The

Jewish section has many remarkable monuments and includes the tombstone for my grandfather who died of natural causes. Aunt Irene arranged to have the names of my parents added to his tombstone which was so important in being a permanent memorial for their lost lives and providing a place to which I and others in the family could go.

I do sometimes think of just how many there are of us here today because of the bravery of my parents. Apart from their three sons of whom two, myself and Jacques are still around, my five wonderful children and eight equally wonderful grandchildren I also have ten nieces and nephews, nineteen great nieces and great nephews, and at the last count fourteen great-great nieces and nephews! A tribe! It is a challenge to try to keep in contact with the ever-expanding family but a joy to do so.

My involvement with the Kindertransport continued to evolve. I became a member of the committee and also represented the Kindertransport on the Association of Jewish Refugees Committee. Amongst the many projects the AJR take responsibility for is a fund which is used specifically to help Austrian refugees living in this country in impoverished or difficult circumstances. Given my Austrian heritage I have been involved with this fund for many years. It so often reminds me how some refugees have never been able to come to terms with what happened to them or to make a new life for themselves.

A little bit more history is required to bring me to another landmark meeting in my life. The Central British Fund (CBF) for German Jewry had been set up in 1933 specifically to support Jews in Germany and Austria and was highly involved in the rescue mission that was the Kindertransport. It is now known as World Jewish Relief (WJR) and to this day does incredible work round the world supporting those in poverty and crisis.

In 2002 HRH the Prince of Wales had visited Krakow. The district of Kazimierz, home to a significant Jewish community up until the Holocaust, made a strong impression on him and in response to the Jewish religious community there he, together with WJR and a similar organisation in America, helped to secure funding for a new Jewish Community Centre for Krakow which he formally opened in 2008.

With the pending anniversary of the end of the war in 2005, Prince Charles liaised with WJR on how they might mark the occasion. WJR suggested the Kindertransport and as a result Prince Charles hosted a reception for Kinder at Clarence House in 2005 which I was invited to attend. It was at this delightful gathering that I was introduced to the renowned sculptor Frank Meisler, himself a Kind. We hit it off instantly. I had hoped to meet him as I had been told of his public art work. The monument to the Kindertransport that had been unveiled at Liverpool Street station in 2003, where I started this odyssey, had by then suffered structural problems and had been dismantled.

Frank agreed to design a new monument called *Kindertransport – the Arrival*. It takes the form of five children of various ages arriving at Liverpool Street Station. The smaller boy standing with a violin case is modelled on a picture of me as a boy. Fame at last!

Frank and I have worked together ever since, Frank designing and finding suitable locations, me trying to raise the finance and the indomitable Lisa Schaefer obtaining permissions. Lisa is a non-Jewish journalist who lives in Berlin where through her inter-faith work she became aware of and involved with us and the Kindertransport.

There are now several monuments in Europe: at the railway station in Gdansk entitled *Kindertransport – the Departure*; at the Friedrichstrasse Station in Berlin entitled *Trains to Life – Trains to Death*; and at the Hook of Holland entitled *Channel Crossing to Life*. It has been an amazing collaboration and has created much-treasured friendships.

In 2009 in Gdansk with sculptor Frank Meisler, unveiling another monument in his Kindertransport cycle, this one called 'The Departure - Danzig 1939'

Millions of families are affected as a result of conflicts going on around the world to this very day and highlighting the Kindertransport may act as a reminder of both the suffering and of the help which can alleviate misery.

Which is why I have always felt it vital for future generations to know in the hope that they will learn and not make the same mistakes. And why I have been so committed to the programme of monuments. I have also been invited to give talks about my story and the Kindertransport – of these the ones I feel are so important are those that I give to school children. They know little if anything about the Kindertransport and find great difficulty in comprehending that my parents could let me go at the age of four, and that I have absolutely no recollection of them whatsoever.

As the years went by we realised that another significant moment was fast approaching – the seventieth anniversary of that momentous decision by Parliament in November 1938 to allow approximately ten thousand children up to the age of seventeen into the country. This was in 2008 and we set about organising a special celebration which was held at the Jewish Free School in North London. By this time, I was the Chair of the Kindertransport and had the honour of not only chairing the day but escorting HRH Prince Charles. He had intimated his wish to attend and be involved but he was only available later in the day so he 'took tea' with the Kinder before making the closing address. He spoke movingly of his paternal grandmother Princess Alice who had sheltered Jewish refugees in Greece during the War.

Sharing a joke with Prince Charles on his visit to a Kindertransport
anniversary reunion

Over five hundred Kinder and their families attended, some coming from as far as America and Israel. Distinguished speakers included the Chief Rabbi, the eminent historian Sir Martin Gilbert, author of Jewish history and of Holocaust books, and Sir Richard Attenborough whose emotional address recalled his parents and their role in taking in two refugees. This, coupled with some great klezmer music and most importantly lots of time for the Kinder to be reunited, talk and catch up, sharing their unique bond, made it an unforgettable day for all of us.

Chapter Fifteen

Liverpool Street Station to Buckingham Palace, aged 4–74

Nor deem the irrevocable past
As wholly wasted, wholly vain
If rising from its wrecks at last
To something nobler we attain

Henry Wadsworth Longfellow

One misty, wet, and rather miserable late November morning in 2009, I rang Linda from the office to tell her I had to pick something up from Muswell Hill. 'Why don't you pop home on your way?' she asked. She seemed unusually insistent and, as I wasn't in a rush, I said OK. Imagine my surprise when I opened the door and found Linda standing in the hallway in tears.

She was holding an opened brown envelope stamped 'On her Majesty's Service' and clearly addressed in large letters: 'Strictly Private and Confidential for Mr Erich Reich'. Linda opening my letters, confidential or otherwise, was not an unusual occurrence – her crying was.

Gently taking the envelope from Linda's hand, and with more than a little trepidation, I slowly drew out the single sheaf of paper it contained. As my eyes scanned it, I became transfixed. *'The Prime Minister wonders if you would be amenable to have your name put forward to the Queen for a Knighthood for services to charity and the Kindertransport.'*

I was dumbfounded. I could not take in what I was reading. It is hard to explain but for at least two days I was in shock and barely able to sleep. I couldn't understand what I'd done to deserve such an honour. Momentarily, I even thought of refusing. This was something totally out of my sphere. It wasn't me at all. Later when I tried to calm down I began to think of all the people who, over the years, had been involved in helping organise and participate in the numerous charity events, and also of the recognition that this would bring to the Kindertransport: the ten thousand children who had arrived on these shores between 1938 and 1939, who had to absorb an alien culture, learn a foreign language and make a new life, far from the love and comfort of their parents, and the contribution that many had subsequently made to this country suddenly struck home. In the event I was proved right; the pride felt by those associated with my knighthood was overwhelming.

Even as I write these words I can feel my heart thumping and my nerves begin to tingle but, above all, I still feel humbled. I haven't really ever stopped asking myself how an orphan who landed on these shores from central Europe just prior to the Second World War, later a kibbutznik and a soldier who served in the Israeli army, could become a knight of the British Realm. Trying to answer is not easy but, before I ponder further, on a lighter note I'd like to take you back to the day of my investiture in May 2010. I shared my big day with 119 other deserving people - all there to receive various honours, including MBEs and OBEs, but only two of us knighthoods. My fellow knight was Nicholas Hytner, the then Director of the National Theatre. I'd never met him before but introduced myself to him and said that I thought he knew my son.

'What's his name,' he asked.

'Allon Reich,' I replied.

'Of course I know him,' he immediately responded.

Allon had worked with Hytner, helping transfer two of the plays he had directed, *The Madness of King George* and *The History Boys*, from stage to screen. I was a very proud dad.

Anyway, we had a special rehearsal to make sure we were aware of the etiquette of bowing one's head when arriving in front of Prince Charles, who was representing the Queen on that day, and then again when leaving, and also, which knee to bend and kneel on. Perhaps it was the combination of not paying enough attention as is often my wont, or the enormity of the occasion itself in the Grand Ballroom of Buckingham Palace, but either way when I found myself in front of Prince Charles I initially got down on the wrong knee.

'I'm glad one of us knows what to do,' Prince Charles whispered.

It was a bit embarrassing, but his response made me smile and relax and helped ease the formality of the rather serious ceremony. We spoke about how he had kindly agreed to attend, as the guest of honour, the seventieth anniversary celebration of the decision by parliament to allow the ten thousand Kindertransport children to enter the UK.

'I followed you, holding your cup of tea and honey, while you talked to the Kinder,' I continued.

'I'm so glad the Kindertransport has at last been recognised,' he responded.

These words alone made it made it even more special to accept the knighthood.

Watching a video of the event a few weeks later, my family were even more amused to note that not only did I stumble over which knee but I also did not take the prescribed step back after I'd been knighted, and did not bow my head as rehearsed. I was lucky not to be sent straight to the tower!

It certainly made me think, yet again, about the many twists and turns that I'd been confronted with throughout my life. How I had survived the Holocaust itself and a few other near misses: my serious accident as a child, later nearly electrocuting myself, the army and the war I fought in. My grandmother giving birth to my father, her youngest of nine, at the advanced age of forty-six in a Polish shtetl in 1900. In many ways, lucky to be here at all.

I thought of the actions I had taken in trying to overcome what seemed at the time insurmountable hurdles that kept appearing in front of me. Strength I may have got from my parents who must have had so much of it to let their three sons go to a foreign land. Actions that might have been attributable to this and other inherited character traits or just instinctive responses but which tended to be short-term solutions rather than well thought-through plans. Many led to pretty unsuccessful outcomes.

Each shift in my life becoming a kind of independent chapter not necessarily linked with the previous one. Many incidents appear like blurred images behind a veiled curtain. Others, unfortunately, have remained vivid and in sharp focus.

Take, for example, the time I disobeyed my foster parents, broke my nose and was hospitalised for weeks. My first concern was whether I was having my tonsils out, like my school friends. When I discovered this wasn't the case, and despite the pain I was in, my mind filled itself with the imagined wonders of the grammar school at which I'd be starting in the autumn. Looking forward to something positive made me forget the stupidity of my actions and the pain, which lasted for several weeks. It never occurred to me that both Sonya and I could have been killed although as a child you don't think about consequences like that.

Having to uproot my life for a second time at the age of fourteen, then not fitting in with the lifestyle of my aunt in Haifa and having to acclimatise to another totally alien way of life in a kibbutz, was certainly not of my making. The solution, Kibbutz Merchavya, was where at least I had a cousin, Eliezer, even if I'd only met him once before and had no idea where exactly he fitted into my family tree.

For the third time in less than fifteen years I had to learn to a new language, and adapt to new cultures and traditions. Kibbutz life was very different to anything I had known. It was complicated for me to absorb and at times it became mentally disorientating and extremely difficult. I had become a young suburban English teenager, who only a decade earlier had left central Europe, not to mention the complications of having to juggle between two religions. What could I do? Get on with it, absorb the new way of life and become a 'kibbutznik'.

This frequent relocating also meant there was never enough time to make close and lasting relationships with my peers, a pattern that has followed me throughout my life.

Perhaps these constant moves explain why later, when working in the travel industry, I never felt afraid to venture to places I didn't know. In fact, I loved exploring, finding new routes, and have been fortunate to have seen some wonderful places in the world. I do not have a fear of the unknown or the unfamiliar. I relied on the kindness of strangers and I put trust in people that I barely knew. As I had done so often in my youth I did this in work, hoping that they would behave in business in an honourable way, as I would. Often this was the case.

I was fortunate to have the most dedicated staff at Classic Tours, totally committed to the aims and ideals of the company, some of whom were with me for many years. I watched them grow with the company, both professionally and personally, then enjoyed seeing some of them embrace motherhood while continuing to work part-time. The Classic Tours team were like a large family that extended way beyond those that work in the office - the tour managers, doctors, mechanics and all the other various support staff as well as the ground-handlers round the world.

With the Classic Tours family after my investiture at Buckingham Palace
May 10th 2010

From the outset, my principal ground-handler was Ayala Tours in Israel and with its representative Yair and his wife Orna, I have forged a special friendship. Classic Tours and the work it has done raising millions of pounds for charities has not only changed the lives of those who benefit from the charities' work but also of those of us who provided the service. When a few years ago Yair celebrated his sixtieth birthday he decided the only way he could do that was to organise a bike ride and trek for all his friends and family to raise money for his chosen charity. We were thrilled to be with him for his party in the hills around Jerusalem – a beautiful day.

Despite everything, I never held the view that all was doom and gloom. Yes, there were moments of despair. With the end of my second marriage which had lasted twenty years I not only had lost family life but also my own home – my sanctuary – that I had worked so hard to achieve. At times my needs, as the result of the ever-changing whirlwind of life, were so overwhelming they frequently drove me to take hasty actions or, more accurately, allowed my emotional needs to take over. But I must emphasise I've also had many moments of great happiness, joy and satisfaction; inspired by family, holiday and work.

I have always had a relentless inner urge for a companion to provide a safe haven and share my life with. I'm sure Freud would have had a multitude of explanations why this urge for close companionship resulted in several marriages; I'd suggest that the rise of Nazism, the Holocaust and the consequent separation from parents at such a young age had the greatest impact. Perhaps the marriage breakdowns stemmed from an over-anxious need to be wanted, to please, to be involved, to maintain equilibrium and keep the family I'd helped create together. All this without the benefit of having grown up with parental role models to show me normal family life. As each chapter closed I found myself in the position in which I least wanted to be; alone, and with the sinking feeling of being abandoned, again and again, and not understanding why.

I am lucky to have a companion now who cares as much about me as an individual, with all my hang-ups and baggage, as I do for her; someone who gives as much, if not more, than takes. The question of compromising just doesn't surface. For both of us, mutual respect and understanding are as natural a function as living and breathing. After so many years, the slim chance of meeting a person who is on a similar wavelength is quite extraordinary. I am not only enjoying retirement but feel a longed-for sense of security and contentment.

With Linda after the investiture ceremony for my knighthood 10th May 2010

Perhaps things could have been different.

If, for example, the Jewish community had not been so insistent on my leaving Dorking for a more religious education I would have completed secondary school there, and maybe even gone on to university which would have offered a profession like teaching that I know I would have been good at. I recall Linda once asking me if there was anything I would like to do if I was free to make a choice. The answer was to go to Cambridge, a city I have always loved, to study history. History has fascinated me since I was a young boy and great lengths of our shelves are taken up with books on the subject. In fact, when I was settled in Muswell Hill I felt the need to study more formally and enrolled with the Open University. I enjoyed it thoroughly and although sadly because of family and work commitments I never managed to finish and get my degree I continue to read avidly to this day.

Undoubtedly, a major setback was the death of my brother, Ossie. It wasn't just his passing away, which was unexpected and terrible, but the fact that he knew I was coming and that I could at least, even if only briefly, have seen and talked to him if I'd been aware of the gravity of his illness. This is a pain I will always carry with me.

This loss of another close family tie probably intensified my search for companionship. It upset my balance and resulted in me trying to help other people, when in reality, I was seeking close friendship, help and stability for myself. The human heart and mind sometimes appear to function at odds with each other. The former in a desperate search for warmth, tenderness and understanding; the latter signalling warning bells, the need for patience and to look before you leap. In my case the former frequently took precedence, consequently leading me into a maze of blind alleyways and not always learning from previous mistakes.

I was exposed to two religions at a young age. Yet even now I have great difficulty in understanding, and thus believing, that there's some heavenly power controlling and supervising the deeds, or misdeeds, of the millions of people in whichever religion into which they may have been born. I do appreciate the fact that many of us desperately need to believe in something to help regulate our lives and feel a sense of security within specific boundaries.

Looking back at my heritage, I've come to believe that though, several thousand years ago the Jewish religion may have been the most innovative and advanced of any at that time and for many years later, to me it seems to have remained static and not progressed much since. Forgetting for a moment the concept of a sole, super heavenly power, the other laws mainly revolved around dietary rules, health issues and agricultural logic at a time when fridges and the like were unavailable.

It may be that the history of anti-Semitism has persuaded many that the survival of the faith is synonymous with maintaining strict adherence to ancient, dare I say outdated, rules when acknowledging the traditions and culture in a simple way could be enough. My religion happens to be based on honesty, truth and, where possible, helping the many in society less fortunate than myself. In other words, a belief in being a normal, decent human being while I'm on this earth. Who knows what, if anything, happens afterwards?

Other constants that have been in my life are music and running, both in my youth and, later, in adulthood. Running allowed me to distance myself from the turbulence around me as well as providing space and time to contemplate ideas and emotions running through my head.

Music not only has a strong calming effect on me but also brings a pervasive sense of wellbeing. I probably inherited my love of music from my father who was a stand-in cantor in Vienna. Apart from being religious, he must have had a pretty good musical voice otherwise it's unlikely he would have had such a role in a Viennese synagogue. Despite not inheriting his standard of singing, nor ever having learned to play an instrument, music has played an important role in my life. Most of my children and grandchildren have learned to play a musical instrument and a few have even been commended on their singing ability. I suppose this talent has simply skipped a generation. Nevertheless, when I'm upset, or feel emotionally stressed, listening to some of the beautiful chords and harmonies created by Beethoven, Mozart and so many other composers, helps to uplift me and rationalise my internal conflicts. Whenever I hear music on the radio my first reaction is to try and identify the piece. If I'm right I breathe a sigh of relief — my faculties are still working.

Now in my eighties I'm aware that I've become a person enriched by my experiences; many unique, and all contributing to the mosaic that is me. I've continually changed my way of life but not my outlook on life. I frequently find myself trying to avoid conflict; not always, I must hasten to add, the appropriate response to the perceived, or otherwise, wrong-doings of others.

The more I look back, the more I begin to understand what a complex species we are, and how differently each individual reacts to circumstances they find themselves in.

My experiences undoubtedly helped broaden my outlook in later life and gave me a wider, more open perspective. They made me realise that people come from diverse backgrounds and, consequently, behave in different ways. Most importantly, they helped me appreciate that even if other cultures don't coincide with my own, their beliefs are not necessarily 'wrong', or shrouded in some evil intent that has to be eradicated. I suppose they also impressed on me the fact that no matter what religion we subscribe to, at the end of the day we all originate from the same human species and are more akin to each other than dissimilar in aspirations and desires.

I know Parliament's decision to allow the Kindertransport was unique and quite extraordinary, but does it deserve greater recognition than the parents who had the courage to let their very young children go, not knowing if they would ever see them again?

I dedicate my story to my wonderful children and the amazing families they are raising, to my parents who I thank for giving me life twice - once when I was born and again when they let me go, and to the Kreibichs who watched over me as I grew up.

With my children: Liora and Allon, on the left and Joel, Rameet and Jonathan on the right, after the Barmitzvah service of my grandson Noah in Summer 2008

Back to Vienna with my two youngest on my
80th birthday at the 'Third Man' museum

My personal thanks to:

Karl French

Tom Kinninmont

Deborah Haase

Sharon Levinson

Berny Winehouse

Lionel Ross

and my lovely wife Linda

for all their help, advice, support and enthusiasm

Erich